SPORTS CARS

Doug Nye

Exeter Books

NEW YORK

Author	**Doug Nye**
Illustrator	**Jim Dugdale**
Editor	**Tim Auger**
Designer	**Ron Pickless**
Consultant	**Michael Ware**

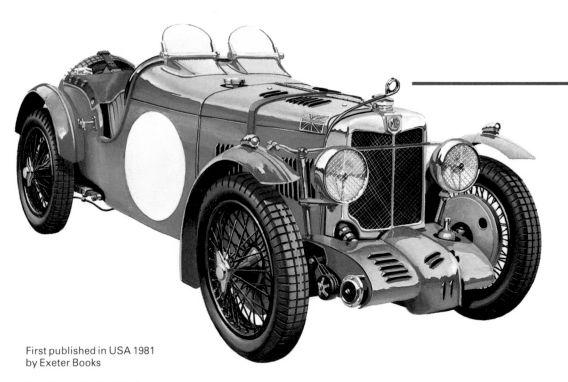

First published in USA 1981
by Exeter Books

Distributed by Bookthrift, Inc
New York, New York

Designed and produced by
Grisewood and Dempsey Limited
141-143 Drury Lane, London WC2
© Grisewood and Dempsey Limited 1980

Color separations by Newsele Litho Ltd, Milan
Printed and bound by South China Printing Co, Hong Kong

ISBN 0-89673-068-9

Contents

Introduction

What is a sports car? That question has been asked innumerable times, and many long and learned essays have been written under that title. One could claim that a sports car is an open two-seater offering high performance both in a straight line, and through corners. But some sports cars have appeared which have roofs and more than two seats and which can out-perform their open roadster brethren not only along the straight, but also through those all-important corners. So we try another answer. A sports car is a high-performance car. Simple as that? Well, no, for some high-performance cars are built very much for straight-line comfort; to carry five people and a mass of luggage a thousand miles or more on motorways, freeways, autoroutes and auto-strada with a minimum of fuss and fatigue. A Citröen-Maserati SM saloon car or a Rolls-Royce Corniche is a high-performance car of this type. With the best will in the world, no enthusiast could adequately describe either of them as a 'sports car'.

Perhaps a sports car is largely indefinable, but those who seek one will recognize it when they see it . . .

For many years the type in essence was virtually unmistakable. Most sports cars would have open cockpits, and most of them would have no more than two seats. The type evolved in the vintage period of the nineteen-twenties and caught firm hold in the thirties in models such as the MG Midget and Magnette. Postwar their descendants, particularly the MG T-series, spelled 'sports car' to the world in an unmistakable manner. Yet the T-series cars in particular, the MG TC, TD and TF of the late forties and early fifties, were never particularly fast cars. What was really important was that they looked fast, they looked sporty, and the people who owned and drove

them with such enthusiasm (despite the miseries of leaking hoods and freezing feet in rain and snow) derived immense *enjoyment* from them. This is perhaps the key. For the sake of enjoyment, for many years men and women took up open-air motoring in a machine which would accelerate more briskly than most bread-and-butter 'transport' cars on the road; which would brake more effectively than them; which might have a higher ultimate top speed in a straight line; and which would especially be capable of negotiating corners safely at a much higher speed. These attributes in turn produced a vehicle admirably well-suited for use in competition events on road or track in addition to humdrum motoring duties. If a car was essentially capable of participating in sporting events, then it could be assumed to be a 'sports car'.

One must have reservations about such a definition, but looking through the following pages the reader will see that the sports cars we have selected do not stray far on either side of a sporting central thread. The earliest 1903 60 hp Mercedes was a high-performance production road car stripped to save weight and entered as a last minute stop-gap in the important Gordon Bennett Trophy race, which it actually won. In this way it proved itself a sporting car of considerable stature, although in essence its design was derived from that of a pure-blooded racer, 'de-tuned' for road use. Here the sports car shows an origin close to that of the Grand Prix car, but this book follows the sports car as it developed along separate lines.

The first true sports-car competition developed in Germany before World War I as the Herkomer Trial, and its successful descendant, the Prince Henry Trial. These events almost unwittingly encouraged interested motor-manufacturers to construct specialized touring cars which combined powerful engines with lightweight body designs and the latest thinking in steering, braking and suspension. Upon the success of the Trial-winning designs, victorious manufacturers would put into small-series production cars which were in many cases sold only to customers of recognized ability! In many cases these carefully allocated sporting cars were destined to undertake extensive sprint and hillclimb competition programmes in order to promote their manufacturers' names and images more widely, and upon their success depended the mass sales of those 'transport' designs – the growing volume of bread-and-butter motor cars designed to transport people and baggage from point A to point B . . . and little more.

After World War I came the vintage years of motoring in Europe and America. This was the period in which the many-faceted 'sports car' market developed, although not under such a glib and modern title. Enthusiast cars ranged from the spartan and often diabolically dangerous cyclecars like the various GNs of Britain and the French Bedélia designs to the middle-of-the-road Alvises, the strikingly neat and fast Amilcars, Salmsons and Bugattis, the dignified but so sophisticated Lancias, to the sporting epitome of their

time – the likes of the Vauxhall 30/98, the Bentleys and the SS-series Mercedes-Benz.

Today each of these cars, even the still-humble but so fascinating little cyclecars, have become much-sought-after collectors' items, cherished by the true enthusiast and salted away by the stone-hearted investor. What most of these classical vintage sports cars have in common is their lack of a fixed roof and their considerable power/braking/ steering/roadholding advantage over contemporary workaday saloon cars. This advantage in these vital departments continued into the thirties although some exceptions, like the saloon-bodied Lancias and the mighty Hispano-Suiza limousines, served to prove the rule. Despite their extra weight both were capable of out-performing many more flashy 'true sports cars' upon otherwise even terms.

During the thirties sports-car racing achieved major importance in events such as the Le Mans 24-Hours in France, the Mille Miglia in Italy and the RAC Tourist Trophy in the United Kingdom. These fostered the design, construction and promotion of such classic sports cars as the Alfa Romeo 8C-2300, the MG 'K3' Magnette, the Talbot 105 and the Delahaye 135C. Each of these great cars is described in detail in the text which follows, and is fixed there in relation to its

The 1937 works team of SS '100' models posed before the year's Welsh Rally.

◀ Bugatti Type 55 hill-climbing in Britain, inside rear wheel spinning, tyre smoking, and no doubt the exhaust note setting every spectator's spine a-tingle. . . .

▼ 1925 Lancia Lambda storming the stony hill at Beggar's Roost during a 'tween-wars Lands End Trial.

sister models from the same manufacturer, and against the background of its contemporary rivals.

The vital thing to remember is that competition models such as these were developed from, and became the prototypes for further development of high-performance sporting cars intended primarily for sale to the general public for use on the open highway. In this vital respect they differed from the highly-specialized purpose-built racing car, which had developed worldwide into a single central-seat open-wheeled projectile by 1932–33 and which in essence was to have decreasing significance for road-car manufacturers as the years rolled by.

Yet in the thirties the sporting car was still essentially a wealthy man's toy, and there is no doubt that the lucky original owners of these cars often played long and hard with them, and derived enormous pleasure from the experience. It was after World War II that such pleasure really began to become available to all, in the mushroom growth particularly of the British sports car industry in which models like the immortal MG T-series, the Triumph TRs, the Austin-Healey family, the mighty Jaguar range and the peripheral marques like the Allards,

HRGs, the true Healeys, Aston-Martins were produced *en masse*. The vast majority of all these British cars were exported, mainly to the USA, and as Britain came to displace Italy from motor-racing domination so this firm foundation of sports-car know-how and commercial success played its part.

Still, the Italian sports car had made its mark through the 'tween-war years and that turbulent nation of flair, imagination and supreme craftsmanship continued to produce sports cars which represent the pinnacle of the art—names like Ferrari, Maserati and Lancia were to have few peers in international road-racing competition, but their products were few and expensive, beyond the pocket of Mr Average, who could easily find the where-withall to indulge his enthusiasm at the wheel of an MG, TR, Healey or 'Jag'.

The success of these marques in all parts of the world was not lost upon General Motors and the Ford Motor Company in America, and in the fifties and sixties both launched their sports car projects—the Chevrolet Corvette family and the Mustang-to-GT40 programme which in both cases had a two-fold effect. Firstly sporting cars were sold to a new-found 'youth' market with the money to pay for fun on four wheels. Secondly these sporting cars in general image and in all manner of competition—from the most humble Sports Car Club of America club race to the International arena of Le Mans—promoted a feeling of endeavour, excitement and achievement which reflected credit throughout the rest of those manufacturers' ranges, however mundane.

By this time the sports car as generally accepted—the open-top two-seat roadster—had begun to lose its performance advantage over the bread-and-butter transport motor car. More competition sporting-car know-how was being built into more cars. Ford of Britain achieved saloon-car racing dominance in Britain and her Commonwealth with successive models from the 105E Anglia through the Cortina to the Escort and Fiesta of today. Alfa Romeo in Italy picked up with the GTA saloon where they had once dominated with the classical 8C-2300; the class of racing had changed, but the success and image of achievement was the same. Jaguar saloon cars for many years were just as dominant in British saloon-car racing as had been their C-Type and D-Type sports-racing sisters in former years at Le Mans. Mercedes-Benz sent saloon cars racing successfully through the Pampas of Argentina and round the looping mountain course of the Nürburgring to emulate the former dominance of their legendary Grand Prix cars, and of the immortal 300SLR sports-racer of the fifties.

Rallying Alpine-Renault.

In each case these were tin-top saloon cars which in standard trim could be seen flowing through (or choking) the streets of any town or city almost anywhere in the Free World. The sixties saw the release of saloon car models like the Ford Lotus-Cortina and the Escort Twin-Cam, which could out-brake and often out-corner many of the classic sports cars of yore, and most of their contemporary pure-bred 'sports car' competition. For example any reasonable Ford Escort saloon would make most MGs or Triumph TRs look positively lame through winding country lanes, and so a form of roofed-in but still pleasurable sporting motoring evolved. This reached its natural conclusion in the development of enclosed-cockpit sports cars, such as the original Triumph TR7, which was hastily designed when it appeared that the burgeoning volume of American Federal Safety Regulations would ban open-cockpit cars, because of their lack of roll-over protection for their occupants. This subsequently proved to be nothing more than scare-mongering, and an open-cockpit TR7 has now been introduced specifically for the lucrative but sensitive American market.

Towards the end of this book, therefore, you will find many roofed-in high-performance cars which qualify for the 'sports car' tag none the less. The Ford Escort is not amongst them; it is a saloon which could undoubtedly in its many and highly individual variants out-perform many of the cars we have included, but such high-priced Grand Touring exotica as the De Tomaso Pantera, Lamborghini Miura and Porsche Turbo demand the space; they are unequivocally 'sports cars' in the most modern sense.

From all this emerges one common theme. The pleasure of motoring, the joy of driving, is best served by those machines we call sports cars – and among their names we find some which by their special appeal, their competition success, their commercial success, or sometimes merely by their unusual technical interest or charm, must qualify for the 'classic' tag.

The arrangement of this book is basically chronological, with the cars in each year placed alphabetically, although there are one or two departures from this rule where it makes sense to group particular cars together, or where a particularly important car merits a two-page spread to itself. In what follows some enthusiasts may be outraged to find that their particular favourite has been omitted in favour of something they consider unworthy, but – like the definition of 'sports car', perhaps – it is all a matter of opinion . . .

The French Matra MS530 was typical of the high-performance sporting car of the seventies – roof and all.

'Gordon Bennett' Mercédès

1903, Germany

In the earliest days of motor-racing competition, the Gordon Bennett Cup was an annual International event contested by carefully chosen national teams of three cars each. The competition was French-dominated until 1902, when Selwyn Francis Edge's Napier was the sole runner to complete the distance from Paris to Salzburg. This British victory gave the Royal Automobile Club of Great Britain and Ireland the right to organize the 1903 event on their home territory. Since it was impossible to gain permission to close public roads on the mainland for motor-racing use, a large figure-of-eight course was chosen near Ballyshannon in what is now Eire.

The Germans produced an excellent racing car in their 90 hp Mercédès model, but just one month before the Irish race took place the Mercédès factory at Canstatt, near Stuttgart, was swept by fire. The racing department was gutted and its 90 hp cars were destroyed. A French Mercédès customer named Baron Pierre de Caters contacted Emile Jellinek, salesman-cum-promoter of the Daimler-built cars which were named after his daughter (Mercédès Jellinek), and suggested that stripped 60 hp production models such as his own might do the job in Ireland. The company took up de Caters's idea, stripped his car of unnecessary fittings and entered him in the Gordon Bennett.

Another 60 hp was called back from American sportsman Clarence Gray Dinsmore. His chauffeur Wilhelm Werner was, however, judged by the German club to be insufficiently qualified as a 'gentleman driver' to represent his country. The Belgian Camille Jenatzy therefore took his place.

At Ballyshannon the two stripped production Mercédès 60s ran very well, and Jenatzy scored Mercédès's first major International victory, averaging 49.2 mph over 327 miles.

Benz 50 hp

1908, Germany

The competitive events which first developed a true 'sports car. breed were organized in Germany before World War I. They were known as the International Touring Car Competition for the Herkomer Trophy. The first competition was sponsored by Professor Hubert von Herkomer RA, one of its prizes being a portrait of the winner painted free of charge by the Professor himself. It began in 1905 and was won by a hefty Mercédès 40 with more or less standard heavyweight coachwork. In 1906, however, coachwork regulations were relaxed and lightweight bodies appeared, to aid the cars' power-to-weight ratio and so improve their performance.

The Prince Henry Benz. notable for its flared wings to become a trademark of later sports cars.

An 18/20hp Horch of only 2.7-litres won.

Herkomer's last competition was run in 1907. One enthusiastic competitor in these pioneering events had been Prince Henry of Prussia – younger brother of the Kaiser – and he presented a trophy for a touring-car event to replace the Herkomer, open to four-seater vehicles, setting engine bore limits and excluding 'trade entrants'. The competition was known as the Prince Henry (actually *Prinz Heinrich*) trial.

The first Prince Henry Trial in 1908 saw exotic 'specials' appearing, far more exotic than Herkomer entrants had ever dreamed of; Horch, for example, ran stark four-seater cars with a cowl separating front and rear passengers, with flared wings but no doors. This type of body became known as the 'torpedo' type, the germ of the sports car. The event was won by Fritz Erle, a faithful Benz dealer and competition driver from Mannheim, driving a 50hp Benz with rather less streamlined coachwork than the Horch competition but still with the flared wings and streamlined scuttle which were to typify later sports cars.

The Prince Henry Trial course included acceleration tests and against-the-clock hillclimbs, and Erle's big Benz was timed at 86mph over a six-mile strip. In common with most other similar cars of the period it was a hefty four-cylinder with chain drive to the back axle, wooden-spoked artillery wheels and brakes only on the rear wheels and on the transmission shaft. It was built to go, not stop.

Stanley
1908, United States

This was among the earliest sporting cars to be built for sale in the United States of America. Steam cars had become widely popular for their silence and good pulling power, but apart from a few highly-tuned 'specials', they had all been fairly staid transport with hardly rib-crushing performance. More and more manufacturers turned away from steam towards the greater power instantly to hand with the internal combustion engine, but in America the Stanley brothers remained faithful to boiling water. For example, they had built an extraordinary World Land Speed Record contender named *Wogglebug* or *The Beetle*, which achieved the extraordinary speed of 127mph on Daytona Beach in Florida before suffering a major accident which the driver, Fred Marriott, was fortunate to survive.

The Stanley company of Newton, Massachusetts, produced three roadster models, all of sporting character and each with stark but very light two-seater bodies. Their Model EX offered an 18-inch boiler and 10hp engine, the Model H a 23-inch boiler and 20hp engine and the Model K a 26-inch boiler and 30hp engine. It was the median Model H which they delightfully named 'The Gentleman's Speedy Roadster'. Each of these models weighed in at under 1700lb and their performance was truly amazing for 1906–08. The Model H in fact laid claim to the title of Fastest Stock Car in the World after being timed at 68.18mph during a 15-mile handicap race on Ormond Beach, Daytona.

One of the Stanley twins, F. E., was once arrested for driving on the public road 'at nearly 60mph' in one of the products which he and his twin F. O. drove so enthusiastically. The story goes that in Court he pleaded not guilty to the charge '. . . of going 60mph. When I passed the officer my speedometer showed I was going 87 miles an hour!'. The judge evidently appreciated the case's promotional value and fined him all of five dollars.

The brothers Stanley were loyal to steam longer than most of their competitors.

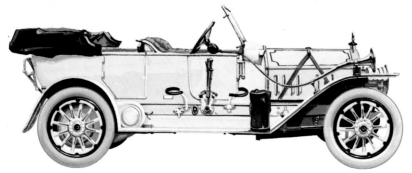

Isotta-Fraschini 100hp
1911, Italy

Fabbrica Automobili Isotta-Fraschini of Milan, Italy, developed from a business partnership between Cesare Isotta and Vincenzo Fraschini. They began producing cars wholely to their own design in 1903 and were soon involved in competition in an attempt to prove their wares.

The 100hp model was probably the most technically interesting high-performance production car of the period when introduced in 1910, and later modified in short-chassis form in 1913. It was a handsome beast with a tall and lengthy bonnet merging into a streamlined scuttle and high-sided, open-top, four-seat bodywork. A raked-back windscreen gave an impression of speed even when the car was stationary, and curvaceous wings merging into long running boards all looked very modern at the time.

Under the bonnet the Isotta-Fraschini was certainly ahead of contemporary practice. The 130mm bore × 200mm stroke engine gave a capacity of 10,618cc and featured a single overhead camshaft operating four valves per cylinder with water pump and ignition magneto driven by skew-gears and shafts from the vertical camshaft drive. This engine delivered some 125bhp. Whereas most of the large overhead-camshaft engines of this period had exposed valve gear and springs the Isotta had a neat cover to cowl in all such essentials. In fact with monobloc fixed-head cylinders and steel water-jackets, affixed by countersunk screws, and separate cylinder bases, it virtually forshadowed the huge $4\frac{1}{2}$-litre Bentley engine to come over a decade later. Isotta also boasted four-wheel braking at a time when front-wheel brakes were widely regarded as a dangerous excess. What was more, Isotta developed a rod control system for their front-wheel brakes which made them consistent and reliable in operation, allowing the power of their car's sophisticated engine to be employed to the full without fear.

Isotta built a little 27/80 sister version of their startling 100, using a 105mm × 180mm 6234cc version of the big 10-litre engine. Both models built a remarkable reputation.

Bédélia Cyclecar
1913, France

Around 1910 there was a move towards inexpensive small-capacity cars with sporting performance, intended to provide a kind of minor competition league and 'fun-car' road use. The expensive big cars were after all available only to the extremely wealthy. Thus appeared the first of the cyclecar genre.

The cyclecars, baby four-wheelers, owed more to motor-cycle practice than to the motor-car world. In Britain the GN made its debut, while in France there appeared the Bédélia. Both were typical.

The Bédélia was developed by Bourbeau and Devaux, setting out with a V-twin engine though later offering singles to order. The

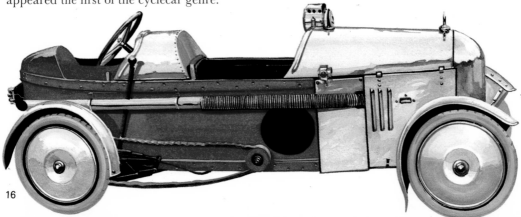

engine was connected by chain to a counter-shaft half-way along the frame, from which final drive to the back axle was by belts. But unlike the GN, which seated its occupants side by side, the Bedélia placed them in tandem in a slimline bodyshell. Steering was by wire-and-bobbin, swivelling the whole front axle in a dangerous manner which most major manufacturers had long since abandoned. But in the lightweight Bedélia the arrangement was good enough for many enthusiastic customers, and since these cyclecars were very cheap to buy, maintain and run, and could achieve around 45 mph as standard and anything up to a dizzy 60 mph when competition-tuned, many were sold.

Bedélias did well in competition as well as on the open road.

Archie Frazer-Nash and H. R. Godfrey built a tiny 'special' powered by a 90-degree V-twin 1100cc JAP engine mounted in line with their chassis, and soon attracted numerous customer orders for replicas. They developed their own engine and with a wooden frame made of ash, and chain-and-belt transmission, their resultant GNs weighed in at little more than 400 lb. Power-to-weight ratio was very favourable and they proved very fast for their size. Latter-day enthusiasts may think that a Morgan or Healey is fairly crude; but for hair-shirt motoring nothing could beat these early cyclecars.

Mercer Raceabout
1913, United States

The Mercer company was named after Mercer County, New Jersey, USA, where it built its cars. It was founded in 1909 as a successor to Roebling-Planche who had made early cars, and members of the Roebling family remained on the Mercer board throughout its peak years. Mercer's chief engineer Finlay Robertson Porter designed the Mercer Type 35 series, which was introduced in 1910 with the Raceabout as its most prestigious model.

The Mercer Raceabout used a modest four-cylinder T-head dual-ignition engine of only 4.9 litres delivering some 60 bhp. The engine was mounted within a very light and simple bodyshell with extremely sporting lines; a bolster tail tank was placed behind two confined bucket seats mounted on an exposed chassis platform with no sides to the cockpit and only an abbreviated engine cowl up ahead. With long flowing wings and running boards the 'Raceabout' tag really described the spirited look of the car. The only concession to weather protection was a circular 'monocle' screen which was available to bolt onto the steering column.

The Raceabouts were fine cars for their day, though their lightweight chassis frames proved susceptible to cracking as the miles mounted up, road ride was very hard and jittery, braking was indifferent at best and wind buffeting was a major problem. However, the Raceabout had all the flair and spirit which was to typify the sports car of a later age, and it sold very well indeed, eventually becoming one of the most sought-after pre-Great War antique cars.

Purebred racing versions of the Type 35 series brought Mercer to the forefront of American competition in these years and when in 1914 Eddie Pullen won the American Grand Prize race for them the whole works was given a half-day holiday. But in 1912 the family scion, Washington Roebling III, had been drowned in the *Titanic* catastrophe and Mercer missed his personal flair and drive. By 1918 the surviving Roeblings had died; and the Mercer company changed hands and its image faded.

'Brescia' Bugatti Type 13
1922, France

The 'Brescia' Bugatti of the twenties was a development of the sensational Type 13 pre-Great War Bugatti model which had performed so strongly in the 1911 'Grand Prix des Vieux Tacots' at Le Mans. The Type 22 became known as the 'Brescia' after its sweeping success in the International 'Grand Prix des Voiturettes' at Brescia in Italy in 1921; it had actually been tested experimentally as early as 1914 in slightly different form.

The modified Type 22 began to achieve fame as a production car in around 1922 and by 1926 it was effectively obsolete; but in those intervening years it was one of the fastest small cars on the market. Ettore Bugatti's overhead camshaft engine of 69mm bore and 100mm stroke, giving the four cylinders a total swept volume of 1496cc, used his famous curved tappets of square section, plus a multi-plate clutch feeding a close-ratio four-speed gearbox. A touring set of gearbox ratios offered speeds of around 40mph, 60mph and 75mph at 3800rpm while in high-geared competition versions maximum speeds rose to 85mph or more. This usually meant that peak engine revolutions could not be achieved in top gear before the engine ran out of steam, and the Brescia would run faster in third. The engines were quoted as giving some 40bhp at 3800 rpm and in sporting trim they weighed around 1340lb.

What was more, the Brescia Bugattis

handled brilliantly for the period with positive steering and high cornering powers which attracted a fanatical band of enthusiast owners. Bugatti insisted that his cars should go and was never very interested in making them stop, so the Brescia's brakes were at best of the 'press hard and pray' variety.

In Britain Raymond Mays dominated sprint and hillclimb meetings in the early twenties with his two famous Brescias, Cordon Rouge and Cordon Bleu, both being progressively and highly modified to achieve 5800rpm with reliability and proving capable of exceeding 90mph with ease.

Morgan Aero
1924, Great Britain

H. F. S. Morgan founded his specialist motor company at Malvern, Worcestershire, in 1910 to produce a unique tricycle car. The single wheel was at the rear of a tubular chassis frame. Up front was a side-valve air-cooled V-twin motor-cycle engine of 1100cc made by JAP. Transmission was by dog clutch and chains, steering was direct and there was independent suspension to each front wheel by sliding pillars and coil springs. There were two simple seats and with reasonable power and light weight this little three-wheeler was capable of considerable performance.

The Morgan proved to have road-holding superior to that of most machines in its class and it rapidly made its name and reputation in sprint and hillclimb events. In 1914 H. F. S.

Morgan introduced his Grand Prix model, the first competition Morgan to be catalogued, and soon afterwards a confined four-seater was unveiled, to become the 'family' model of the twenties.

By March 1919 the little factory at Malvern Link was turning out about 20 cars a week, and through the twenties various engines were used including MAG, JAP and Blackburne. Overhead-valve engines were introduced in 1923 and standardized by 1925. By 1927 the Morgan Aero (introduced with Blackburne engine in 1921) could achieve a genuine passenger-petrifying 80 mph while at more modest touring speeds would return 45 mpg. The Morgan was inexpensive to buy, maintain and run, and its high-speed performance and vast competition pedigree made it the object of almost fanatical love for many enthusiasts.

Lancia Lambda
1925, Italy

Vincenzo Lancia's Lambda model set new standards of handling in 1921–22. Lancia himself had been an electrifying racing driver to watch in the Heroic Age of racing, but after retiring to build production cars he steered clear of competition. He was nevertheless a constructor who enjoyed driving–and this showed in his products just as much as it does with enthusiast managements today, notably BMW and Opel in Germany.

The Lancia Lambda inherited a narrow-angle 'V' engine with overhead camshafts –though in four-cylinder form–from its immediate antecedent, the V8 Lancia Trikappa. The chassis-cum-body was constructed on unitary principles, way ahead of its time, and employed independent front suspension of vertical coil-spring type, as found on all Lancia models until 1956 and present within their range as late as 1963. The Lambda also featured such 'revolutionary' ideas as alloy cylinder blocks, pump cooling, full-pressure lubrication, vacuum fuel feed and four-wheel brakes–all rolled into the one package. Unitary construction with a propeller tunnel for the transmission shaft allowed the Lambda body to be built unusually low for its day, and with powerful cable brakes and 2120 cc engine giving 50 bhp at 3000 rpm the new Lambda was a remarkably exciting innovation. Its wheelbase was too long to make the most of its nimble handling potential but the model proved a great success.

The Lambda was built in eight series until 1931; for the seventh in 1927 engine dimensions were changed from 75 mm bore × 120 mm stroke to 80 mm × 120 mm (2.4 litres), and in 1928 the final models offered 92 mm bore 2.5-litre power units. The standard torpedo touring body was continued little changed through these years with a detachable hard-top available for conversion into a saloon. Early numbers could exceed 70 mph, the later ones 80 mph, but what was more important was their remarkable road manners: smooth riding, controllable and comfortable.

3-litre Bentley
1926, Great Britain

The 1919 London Motor Show was highlighted by the appearance of Walter Owen Bentley's prototype sports car, which carried his own name. W. O. Bentley had been British importer of the DFP car which pioneered aluminium pistons, and during World War I he had designed a string of BR rotary aero-engines. The first sports car carrying his own name had an 80 mm × 149 mm four-cylinder single-overhead-camshaft engine with fixed cylinder head and dual-magneto ignition; it delivered some 70 bhp in prototype form. In the 1922 RAC Tourist Trophy race on the Isle of Man the factory team of three flat-radiator Bentley 3-litres finished 2nd, 3rd and 5th, and in 1924 Duff/Clement won the prestigious Le Mans 24-Hour Grand Prix d'Endurance for the Cricklewood concern. In 1927 the Davis/Benjafield 3-litre Bentley, 'Old No 7', won again at Le Mans after being severely damaged in the extraordinary 'White House Crash' which wiped out the rest of the Bentley team. Up to 1929 Bentley 3-litre production totalled 1630 cars of which a large proportion survive as collector's pieces today.

In 1924 the model had received front-wheel brakes and Vanden Plas – the coachbuilding company – had also introduced their famous sports four-seater 'Speed Model' on this chassis. Red-enamelled radiator badges signified the 'Red Label' Speed Model short-chassis 3-litre Bentley; blue enamelling the

The classical 3-litre Bentley of the vintage years was noted for its high build and 'Gothic' radiator.

early short and long chassis which could and occasionally did carry limousine coachwork. Green enamelling indicated the very special, short-chassis 100 mph type made in restricted numbers.

Of all the vintage Bentleys the 3-litre is perhaps the most graceful and least truck-like with its tall radiator profile and spare

and subtle lines. Its simple 'four' carried 16 valves in pent-roof combustion chambers demonstrating their designer's faith in the pre-World War I Peugeot Grand Prix cars, as did the stroke-to-bore ratio of some 2:1. The Bentley's single overhead camshaft and valve gear was similar to that which W.O. had studied on the 1914 Grand Prix-winning Mercedes, whose engine was in many ways decades ahead of its time. Bentley recognized its merit and improved upon it.

He designed reliability into what Ettore Bugatti referred to caustically as 'the world's fastest lorries'. He spent hours refining his drawings and production methods to ensure that features such as crankshaft support, cooling and overall ease of maintenance were honed to the ultimate degree. On such care and attention to detail he forged Bentley's matchless sustained performance on road and track.

While the Speed Model could cruise at 85 mph in standard form and be tuned to produce 100 mph virtually all day long, it could equally well pull at 8 mph in top gear, and average a fuel consumption of 21 mpg. No wonder the 'old 3-litre' proved such a magnificent beast during its heyday.

At Le Mans for the 1926 24-Hours race, Bentley fought hard to prevent Lorraine winning for the second year in succession. The British marque had won in 1924 but this 3-litre model crashed when third with only 20 minutes to run. It was shared by 'Sammy' Davis and Dr. Benjafield; in 1927 'Old No 7' won the French classic after surviving the infamous 'White House Crash', again shared by this experienced pair.

Vauxhall 30/98 OE
1926, Great Britain

Before World War I the Vauxhall Motor Company was very active in competition and gained a great reputation under the technical guidance of its youthful and dynamic Chief Engineer, Laurence Pomeroy. With the backing of chief executive Percy Kidner, Pomeroy had developed the Prince Henry three-litre and later four-litre high-performance touring model in 1912–13. The larger engine did not give Vauxhall the competition edge they envisaged, and so the 25 hp four-litre engine was given a bore and stroke of 98 mm × 150 mm to provide 4525 cc: the resultant car was named the 30/98.

John Higginson, a well-known textile engineer from Stockport, Cheshire, scored many early sprint and hillclimb successes for the new model and about a dozen replica 30/98s were delivered before the Great War demanded all production capacity.

In the early twenties the Vauxhall 30/98 was indisputably England's premier sporting car. Developed from the stark pre-war competition specials, it carried full road equipment and eventually the famous Velox four-seater body—this combined four seats with slim-line looks of unusual grace and subtlety. The engine was still the Edwardian fixed-head unit with side valves and a single Zenith carburettor, but it delivered a reliable and honest 90 bhp at 2800 rpm and Vauxhall could claim to have the fastest car then available in standard production. The stock model could achieve 85 mph on the public road, while with a racing body a 100 mph Brooklands lap was guaranteed. Several owners

Vintage sporting profile: the Vauxhall 30/98 with four-seater touring body.

Classic Vauxhalls of the vintage era, recognizable by their subtly fluted bonnets, built upon the design and engineering expertise of Laurence Pomeroy and drew upon a background of pre-Great War competition experience. They were aimed not only at the British RAC Tourist Trophy but also the mighty Grand Prix de l'ACF.

insisted on putting this claim to the test, and were satisfied with the result. The car was high-geared, as were most of its genre, and 65 mph cruising was very comfortable and relatively quiet at a lazy 2000 rpm.

The Vauxhall catalogue described the model as 'a very refined fast touring car capable of high average speeds and suitable for competition work'. The manufacturers were justified in claiming refinement for the car; the rest of this description still holds good as the standard by which sports cars of the world should be judged.

In order to achieve greater flexibility throughout the rev range the E-Type engine was modified in 1922 as the 'OE 30/98', offering a shorter stroke and pushrod-operated overhead valves. For 1923 it became a high-speed engine, revving to 3500 rpm, at which speed it produced 112 bhp, compared to the E-type's 90 bhp at 2800 rpm. A counter-balanced crankshaft improved matters still further in 1926 when the boat-tailed 2–3-seat Wensum body style was introduced. It was handsome and rakish, but never replaced the Velox four-seater in the public's esteem.

By 1926 Vauxhall 30/98s had captured something like 13 firsts, 19 seconds and seven thirds at Brooklands Motor Course alone, and OEs added 14 firsts, nine seconds and seven thirds there. Vauxhall kept in close touch with customers who raced their products until in 1926 the American General Motors Corporation bought the English company; the marvellous 30/98 remained in production for just as long as it took to convert the plant for the production of more mundane vehicles of greater mass appeal.

Vauxhall 30/98 at a British Vintage Sports Car Club driving-tests meeting in recent years; a big car to throw around the pylons but more nimble and controllable than it looks.

Alvis 12/50
1927, Great Britain

T. G. John of Coventry, England, founded his Alvis car-manufacturing company in 1919. In 1923 John's chief engineer Captain G. T. Smith-Clarke produced the pushrod overhead-valve 12/50 engine which was quieter and more powerful than its immediate predecessors and coincidentally added remarkable strength and reliability. Alvis won the Brooklands 200-Mile race of 1923 with this engine in tuned competition form, and touring 12/50s entered production with 1598cc engines. The Super Sport versions had a shorter stroke giving only 1496cc, but allowing higher revolutions and more power. While the touring cars could run up to 60–65 mph, the tuned Super Sports could achieve well over 70 mph on the straight and level. Works driver Major C. M. Harvey's victory in that 1923 200-Miles race had formed the perfect base from which Alvis could launch their new model, for he had averaged no less than 93 mph for the distance, and his special car's fuel consumption was a remarkable 24 mpg.

While the company endured various vicissitudes during the mid-twenties, the 12/50 Alvis cars went on to establish a remarkable popularity and they continued in production until 1932. During that period various differing body styles were adopted, the chassis was stiffened, the separate engine subframe was replaced and, in 1924, front-wheel brakes were adopted.

1925 Alvis 12/50 'Duck's Back' in the Land's End Trial.

Although the 12/50 was fairly expensive during its run it sold in larger numbers than any other comparable British 1½-litre car. Many survive and are in regular use today. They are a practical proposition for the impecunious 'Vintagent' and still prove themselves to have been well made to a sound and reliable original design.

'Brooklands' Riley Nine
1927, Great Britain

The Riley Cycle Company of Coventry, Warwickshire, built their first car as a small single-cylinder voiturette with belt-drive. It did not enter production. In 1900 they began production in a modest way, building motor tricycles; tricars with simple engines continued in production until 1907. Later models used a 1034 cc V-twin engine and it was this unit which powered the first four-wheeled Riley cars. Through the twenties Rileys grew in sophistication and performance and in 1927 there was even a supercharged version of the Redwing available.

Then Percy Riley introduced his advanced and sophisticated Nine model. The prototype Riley Nine was announced in the summer of 1926 and justifiably caused a sensation. Its engine was a 1087 cc, 32 bhp four-cylinder unit in which the camshafts controlling valve opening were situated high in the engine flanks but not overhead, actuating the inclined valves through short pushrods, combined with a cylinder head featuring hemispherical combustion chambers–known as the 'PR Head' after Percy Riley himself. This unit was to remain the basis of Riley production until as late as 1957. By the end of 1926 the great Welsh driver-engineer J. G. Parry Thomas was working on the Brooklands sports version of the Riley Nine, and after Parry Thomas died attacking the Land Speed Record at Pendine Sands in March 1927 the work was continued by Reid Railton.

The Brooklands Nine became the epitome of the British sports car, with low-slung and rakish lines, an almost horizontal steering column and flaring front wings. The specialist firm of Thomson & Taylor assembled the first few cars actually at Brooklands, but Riley later took over production themselves. With high-compression pistons and high-lift cam profiles the Brooklands' power was boosted from the Touring Nine's 32 bhp to 50 bhp at 5000 rpm. The Brooklands Nine could achieve 80 mph easily, making it a true match for the French Salmson and Amilcar opposition, and it was to achieve a long and noble record of competition success.

Non-standard approach to the Ards TT pits in Ulster, demonstrated during the 1928 race by this Riley Nine.

Amilcar CGS
1928, France

Messrs Lamy and Akar – motoring enthusiasts and financiers – founded their Société Nouvelle pour l'Automobile Amilcar at St-Denis, France, in 1921. Lamy contracted an engineer named Edmond Moyet to design in detail what became one of the most famous and most successful of all the French voiturette marques which proliferated after the Great War.

Moyet laid out a simple four-cylinder side-valve engine which was used in his three pilot studies, the Amilcar Types CC, CS and 4C; but in 1924 the Amilcar CGS – 'Grand Sport' – appeared with a 1074 cc engine employing full-pressure lubrication in place of the original drip or splash feed, plus front-wheel brakes and half-elliptic front springs. In 1926 this CGS model was developed into the more powerful and lowered CGSS ('Surbaissé') model, and while some touring models were produced it was upon the CGS and CGSS competition sporting cars that Amilcar based its burgeoning reputation.

In 1922 one of the original cars, with dippers on the flywheel flinging oil into a lubrication gallery to feed the bearings, had won the inaugural Bol d'Or race – the first 24-Hours in Europe, preceding Le Mans by one year. By 1924 a separate competition department had been established at the Amilcar factory and the 1100 cc models won innumerable sprints, hillclimbs and bush-league races.

High-built but brisk Frenchman – the 1920s Amilcar series won a vast following in those vintage years, going well and handling tolerably despite their height.

The Amilcar chassis in its CGS form was outstanding for the time but the engine was outmoded by 1925, when Moyet introduced a Delage-inspired 1100 cc engine with twin overhead camshafts, six cylinders, bore and stroke of 44 mm and 77 mm respectively, and Roots supercharging. It gave 83 bhp at 6000 rpm and was installed in a lowered and strengthened chassis frame. Named the G6, this model was catalogued in 65 bhp detuned road trim, but 100 mph was guaranteed! In racing form the car was virtually invincible, 50 were laid down for production in 1926 and in 1927 one special model became the first 1100 cc car to exceed 200 km/h (125 mph) on the road. After 1929 Amilcar decided to make small luxury cars, and so lost their way . . .

Auburn 8/88 Speedster
1928, United States

The Auburn Automobile Company of Auburn, Indiana, USA, was founded by Frank and Morris Eckhart of the Eckhart Carriage Co., situated in that town. Essentially Auburn products were fairly staid and reliable and up to 1924 production seldom exceeded 4000 units a year – small beer by American standards.

In 1924 Errett Lobban Cord bought the business and set about establishing Auburn in the forefront of American high-quality car constructors. He called in J. M. Crawford to redesign the entire model range and in 1925 Auburn offered four-, six- and eight-cylinder models with two-tone colour schemes, striking styling features and a growing reputation for good workmanship and mechanical efficiency.

The four-cylinder baseline model was dropped in 1927 and in 1928 the sporting Auburn Speedster model was released, using alloy pistons and con-rods, larger valves and high-lift camshafts in its Lycoming $4\frac{1}{2}$-litre straight-eight engine, to produce around 90 bhp. The boat-tail body style was attributed to Count Alexis de Sakhnoffsky whose florid artistry was also adopted by the associated marques of Cord and Duesenberg. The Auburns were regularly seen in competition, notably running against Stutz of Indianapolis and nearly always being beaten by them, but the Speedster was much cheaper than the Stutz and always offered a great deal of style and very adequate performance for little capital outlay.

Lycoming V12-cylinder engines were adopted and in two-seater Speedster form the Auburns were guaranteed to achieve 100 mph. The $4\frac{1}{2}$-litre eight-cylinder had a two-speed rear axle which gave effortless high-speed long-distance cruising, but the typically American willow-soft suspension and low-geared steering made the model quite a handful under European road conditions.

Americana – florid styling for the 1931–32 Auburn 8 Speedster.

Mercedes-Benz 38/250 'SS'
1928, Germany

The great German marques Mercédès and Benz merged in 1926 and in that year former Austro-Daimler designer Ferdinand Porsche unveiled for them their Model K. This was an overhead-camshaft 6.2-litre six-cylinder sports car in which full depression of the throttle pedal engaged a supercharger to force-feed the engine. Performance and sound volume increased jointly when the 'blower' cut in, 0–50 mph acceleration in around 30 seconds being improved to 20 seconds by flooring the throttle in this way. The car was good for 95 mph and was a prime example of sheer engine size and then supercharging being used as a means of improving performance.

The high-rigged K models proved difficult to handle, and in 1927 the S or 'Sports' variant appeared, with a lowered chassis line and a 98 mm × 150 mm 6789 cc engine; it offered 120 bhp at 3000 rpm unblown, or 180 bhp with the supercharger engaged. The K's brakes had been improved for the 105 mph 'S' by the use of servo-assistance, and S models were placed 1–2–3 in the 1927 German Grand Prix at Nürburgring.

In 1928 the 'SS' appeared, using a 100 mm × 150 mm 7069 cc twin-carburettor super-charged engine delivering 200 bhp; in stock form under favourable conditions this 2½-ton monster could achieve a genuine 110 mph.

However, the massive chassis of the SS was intended also to accept staid touring coach-work and the 'SSK' – K for *kurz* (short) – was developed as a lightweight short-chassis competition variant with strictly two-seat body-work and a larger-capacity supercharger. In one of these mighty cars Caracciola won the 1929 Tourist Trophy race at Ards. For 1930 a handful of lightened 'SSKL' – *leicht* (lightweight) – models were produced delivering around 300 bhp and capable of as much as 130 mph.

The 'great white Mercedes' achieved major and minor competition success all over Germany and Europe into 1932 and despite their brute force, ignorance was never resorted to in other aspects of their design. They were truly great, classic sports cars, and the Caracciola/Werner performances in the Mille Miglia around Italy and Le Mans 24-Hour races bear testimony to this fact.

Rudolf Caracciola breaking the Semmering mountain-climb record in 1928 in Austria, driving his works Mercedes-Benz 'SSK'.

Francis, the Earl Howe, storms Shelsley Walsh hill-climb in his Mercedes-Benz 38/250 'SS' – quite a sight for the large crowds which flocked to the English venue in the early thirties.

All the K- and S-series cars used the same supercharged single-overhead-camshaft six-cylinder engine varying only in minor details and in capacity. Block and crankcase were a single light-alloy casting, which was quite daring in those days. The camshaft and all the auxiliaries were shaft-driven from the crank. Despite its size and apparent complication this was a fairly simple engine upon which to work, and has been described as a stolid workhorse rather than a highly-strung thoroughbred.

The cars' greatest fault was their inability to stop – their brakes were inadequate relative to their great power, weight and straight-line performance. Nevertheless, even the long-chassis cars handled and cornered well for their time. Much of these cars' development may be credited to Dr Hans Nibel, Benz chief engineer prior to their 1926 merger with Mercedes, and his refinement of Dr Porsche's original design certainly made the series the immortal success they became. Nibel went on to produce other classic Mercedes, the production 500K/540K/770K series with coil-sprung rear swing axle suspension, the rear-engined Type 170, and the original W25 Grand Prix Mercedes of 1934 – the dawn of Mercedes-Benz's greatest era.

▼ *Mercedes-Benz 'SSK', devised by Dr Porsche of later Auto Union and wartime tank fame, and the apotheosis of 'vintage' sports-racing-car ferocity, looked every inch the monster it could be to drive.*

Tulipwood Hispano-Suiza
1929, France

The Swiss engineer Marc Birkigt was responsible for the high-quality Hispano-Suizas
which were among the exotic supercars of
their day, equivalent to the Lamborghinis
and Ferraris seen now.

The first Hispano-Suiza was built in 1904
in Barcelona, Spain, and was actually a
Birkigt-designed 20 hp Castro car renamed. A
range of beautifully built and very sophisticated Hispanos flowed thereafter from Birkigt's
drawing board. All were conventional but
highly developed and very expensive cars and
by 1907 they were found in the garages of
King Alfonso XIII of Spain. In 1910 an
Hispano-Suiza voiturette won the important
Coupe de l'Auto voiturette competition in
France, and from 1911 Hispano production
began in a new French factory in Levallois-
Perret. This very modern plant produced,
in 1919, the stunning H6b to cater for France's
luxury car market, very much larger than that
available in Spain.

The H6b was designed from the ground up
as the ultimate road transport for the wealthy,
using an aero-engine-derived light-alloy six-
cylinder power unit of 6.6-litres with single
overhead camshaft, two valves per cylinder
and a seven-main-bearing pressure-fed crankshaft. With 135 bhp at 3000 rpm in a light yet
rigid chassis, and using four-wheel brakes
designed to control an 85 mph top speed with
ease, the H6b qualified as one of the earliest
Grand Touring cars—its performance put it
into the sporting league despite its luxurious
furnishing and equipment. It did not have

the quiet refinement of a Rolls-Royce, yet it
could out-perform virtually any Rolls with
one wheel tied behind its luggage trunk, and
Hispano-Suiza effectively pursued a one-model
policy based on it for many years.

Salmson 10-20 hp
1929, France

The Emile Petit-designed cars from the
Société des Moteurs Salmson of Billancourt,
France, made a tremendous reputation for
themselves in the 1920s. Salmson had been
renowned for their aero engines during
World War I and in 1919 turned to car manufacture by taking a licence to produce
British GN cyclecars. They built 3000 GNs;
then, in 1921, their own first models appeared
with a flimsy cyclecar-type chassis and an
1100 cc monobloc four-cylinder engine, in
which a single valve-gear control rod per
cylinder operated as a pushrod to open the
exhaust valve and reversed duty as a 'pull'-rod
to operate the inlets.

For the Cyclecar Grand Prix of 1921
Emile Petit introduced a twin-overhead-
camshaft version of this engine and Lombard
won the race with it, and was then second
behind a GN in the 200-Miles Race at Brooklands. In 1922 Salmson cars were placed
first and second in both these events; in 1923
they won their class at Le Mans and went on
to achieve enormous competition success.

From 1925 the twin-cam 1100cc Salmson sports cars took a grip on their competition class and with a cowled radiator from 1926 their classical shape became synonymous with sporting achievement. All the sports models were available with balloon tyres, front-wheel brakes and back axles with no differential. The Grand Prix model had a three-speed gearbox and splash lubrication for its two-bearing crank to achieve 70mph top speeds, while the GP Special used Cozette supercharging, four speeds and pressure lubrication, and was capable of 90mph or more.

Like Amilcar, however, Salmson suffered when MG's low-priced Midget became generally available and under-cut them in the French small-sports-car market. Salmson headed up-market, as did Amilcar. After surviving World War II, Salmson lingered on until 1957, when it was acquired by Renault.

Austin Seven Ulster
1930, Great Britain

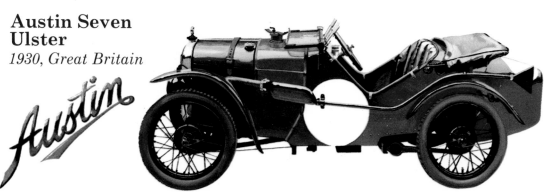

Of all the touring cars which spawned successful competition variants perhaps the diminutive Austin Seven was the most humble.

With its FN motor-cycle-derived engine producing only 13hp and a chassis frame similar to that of the Peugeot 'quad', this unprepossessing little model at least offered four-wheel brakes. At only 747cc the Austin Seven was eligible for the 750cc competition class, in which it faced little opposition. Herbert Austin saw the opportunity for competition prestige on which to sell his production model, and as early as 1924 his company offered a Sports Model Seven with pointed tail, 960lb weight and 52mph.

E. C. Gordon England 'breathed' upon the Sports Model Seven to great effect, producing the 55mph 'Cup' model, and then a very spartan but rapid road-racer which he named the Brooklands. A Cozette-supercharged Super Sports model was introduced by Austin themselves in July 1928, offering 33bhp and no less than 70mph. In the 1929 Tourist Trophy at Ards in Ulster Captain Archie Frazer-Nash finished third on handicap in one of these cars behind Rudolf Caracciola's 7.1-litre Mercedes-Benz and Giuseppe Campari's 1.5-litre Alfa.

In 1929 the Austin Seven Ulster was made available to the public in supercharged and unsupercharged forms, and in the words of one sports car expert, 'serious attention was given to the normally unconventional roadholding of the car and the brakes were also caused to work'–coupling together the four-wheel brakes, which had formerly been activated up front by the foot pedal and at the rear by a hand-brake. The little 747cc engine would rev to 5000rpm and with a close-ratio three-speed gearbox and weight as low as 1200lb top speed was way above 70mph.

4½-litre 'Blower' Bentley
1930, Great Britain

In 1927 the Bentley 3-litre was developed into a 4½-litre variant–still with four cylinders–and development pushed its output up ultimately from 100 bhp to 130 bhp. In 1928 Barnato and Rubin drove a 'four-and-a-half' to victory at Le Mans to underline Bentley's grip on this trial of endurance and speed.

Meanwhile Sir Henry 'Tim' Birkin decided that to achieve optimum performance from W.O.'s design, supercharging should be adopted. The original designer never approved of supercharging as a method of obtaining increased power, always following the dictum that 'there is no substitute for cubic inches'–when he required more urge he preferred to enlarge the engine capacity.

The Hon. Dorothy Paget financed Birkin's plan for a supercharged 4½-litre Bentley and the cars were modified in her premises at Welwyn. The resultant 'Blower Bentley' developed a staggering 240 bhp at 4200 rpm but proved unreliable and incapable of translating that power into race victories. The supercharger operated well at consistently high speeds, such as those achieved on the Brooklands Outer Circuit banking, and there Birkin's very special single-seater version excelled.

A total of 54 'Blower' Bentleys were built, the vast majority for sale as road cars.

We cannot leave these great sporting Bentleys without mentioning two other models of these late 1920s. In 1926 W. O. Bentley had aimed his sights at the luxury market by introducing a 6½-litre six-cylinder chassis upon which the great coachbuilders of the day could weave their magic. Unfortunately the sporting image of the 3-litre Bentley was

Amherst Villiers' supercharger on the nose typified the 1930–31 'Blower' Bentley.

looked at rather disdainfully by the luxury coach customer, and the 6½ was more successful in 1929 in the guise of the 180 hp 'Speed 6'–for many enthusiasts the best Bentley ever made, bringing the company its fourth and fifth Le Mans victories, in 1929 (driven by Barnato/Clement) and 1930 (Barnato/Kidston).

The depression year of 1930 was to bring the collapse of Bentley Motors, and their largest model–the 8-litre six-cylinder car–was cut short in its prime, only 100 being sold before take-over by Rolls-Royce and the loss of Bentley's independent identity.

OM
1930, Italy

SA Officine Meccaniche of Brescia, Italy, was a locomotive-constructor which absorbed the Züst concern in 1918 and built the Züst 25/35 hp car into 1923. OM introduced their own parallel designs, by Barratouché.

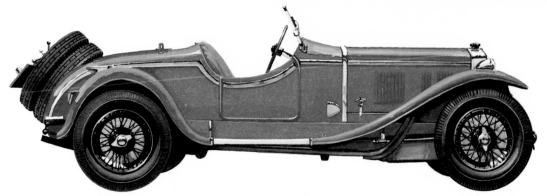

In 1920 a four-cylinder side-valve tourer was joined by the Tipo 665 Superba, a 1991 cc six-cylinder. While the little 'four' had no sporting claims, the two-litre built a surprising motor-racing reputation despite side valves and, normally, a single carburettor.

In 1926 at Le Mans, six-cylinder OMs came fourth and fifth, and in the first Mille Miglia race, in 1927, OM cars came first, second and third. In the 1928 Mille Miglia an OM was second behind an Alfa Romeo 1500. In 1928 Barratouché introduced a low-chassis OM which at least looked sporting and in 1929 its standard six-cylinder engine was enlarged to 2.2 litres. With a Roots supercharger this unit delivered 60 bhp at 4000 rpm. For 1931 its stroke was lengthened to provide a displacement of 2.3 litres, but no OM could now match the contemporary Alfas and Bugattis.

Talbot 105
1931, France

During the 1930s the London factory of Talbot Motors was directed with unerring technical sophistication and skill by Georges Roesch. He had saved the company in 1926 by his introduction of the touring 14/45 Light Six model, which suffered only from being grossly overweight for its 1660 cc engine. In 1930 an enlarged 2.2-litre version was introduced, which was known as the Talbot 90, and this became renowned for its smoothness and silence, its exquisitely made and carefully inspected seven-main-bearing crankshaft, and its excellent road manners up to a top speed of at least 80 mph.

Fox & Nicholl Ltd, the London Talbot agents, fielded a beautifully prepared team of lightened sports-racing '90s' from 1930 to 1933 and with 93 bhp at 4500 rpm in continued smoothness and silence they finished third and fourth behind the Bentleys at Le Mans in 1930, and won their class in the TT, Irish Grand Prix and Brooklands 500-Miles Race. Talbot found themselves once again in the front rank of high-quality sports cars and in 1930 Roesch introduced the 2969 cc 75 mm bore × 112 mm stroke Talbot 105 model giving 100 bhp as standard or 140 bhp in competition tune. Performance was outstanding for an unsupercharged car, particularly one of such refinement.

In 1932 the team of Talbot 105s carried off the team prize in the Alpine Trial, and one car was third at Le Mans in 1932. Mike Couper's special Brooklands version (later fitted with a 3.3-litre '110' engine) achieved over 135 mph and lapped Brooklands at 129.7 mph.

When Sunbeam collapsed in 1935, Talbot – a related company – was dragged to its knees, and the Rootes Brothers takeover resulted in the sweeping aside of all the standards which Roesch had set for himself and his marque, and of those to which his faithful work-force had built the cars.

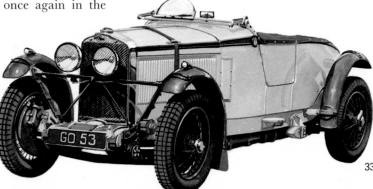

1931 Talbot 105, designed by the famous Georges Roesch.

Bugatti Type 55
1932, France

Bugatti progressed with the Brescia Type 22 model from strength to strength during the twenties, their classical cars excelling in everything from Grand Prix competition through endurance sports-car and touring-car racing to outright production road use. In the Type 55 model Ettore Bugatti produced one of the finest sports cars in history. This model was powered by a variant of the Type 51, 2.3-litre engine with supercharging and twin overhead camshafts; this was a Grand Prix racing engine, installed slightly de-tuned in a Type 54 Grand Prix racing chassis. As a racing project the Formule Libre Type 54 had been shelved after proving itself good for 140 mph or more; but it suffered from poor weight distribution and the deleterious effects which that has on handling and roadholding behaviour. The 4.9-litre engines earmarked for the Type 54s had been diverted to the Type 50T touring models, whereupon the Type 55 came into being to absorb the chassis design, with the smaller and lighter 'two-three' straight-eight-cylinder engine installed.

Topped by beautifully profiled flaring-wing bodywork, the Type 55 Bugatti made a glorious roadster with all the scintillating performance and road manners one might expect from such direct Grand Prix parentage. In first gear the model could top 50 mph, in second it was good for 75 mph, it could clip 100 mph in third and achieved as much as 115 mph in top gear–in absolutely standard tune. It accelerated from 0–60 mph in around 11 seconds, which is sufficiently good to see off many 'sporty' cars in the seventies!

The Type 55 has been described as a true connoisseur's Bugatti with the reservations that it was noisy–as one might expect, and that it was also very stiffly suspended and therefore gave quite a hard ride. With the Type 57 series which followed, *le Patron* set out to put these 'shortcomings' right.

Le Mans Stutz
1932, United States

It was in 1914 that Harry C. Stutz's Indianapolis-based company introduced what became possibly the most famous American motor car of the vintage period–the Stutz Bearcat.

The Stutz sporting car offered the customer a choice of six- or four-cylinder engines, both very large; the former displaced 377 cubic inches (6178 cc) and the latter 390 cubic inches (6391 cc). With a top speed up around 85 mph and rakish styling with, it was said, 'everything that wouldn't rust, including the passengers, out in the open', the Bearcat creamed off much of the former Mercer Raceabout market. In 1915 the works racing Bearcats were fitted with overhead camshafts and four valves per cylinder, even though Harry C. Stutz rapidly lost interest in his competition programme and in fact sold his company in 1919.

From 1920 the Stutz marque continued with cars based on the pre-war designs, improving them in detail from year to year. In 1924 the Speedway Six was introduced as the first overhead-valve pushrod-engined model, and in 1926 the first overhead-

camshaft, eight-cylinder emerged as the Series AA. Stutz resumed racing in 1927 and the AA was extensively modified to suit. The Stutz Black Hawk (named after the Indianapolis factory) dominated American stock-car racing in this period while Miller track-racing cars were entered under Stutz's name and had a fine season in 1928. That year Brisson's Le Mans Stutz was a Model BB, bored out and modified from the AA, and in 1929 the BB was replaced by the further bored-out Model M. A team of three returned to Le Mans in 1929, while Brisson's additional car

had a Roots-type supercharger mounted between its front dumb-irons. Two of the Stutzes split their fuel tanks, a third placing fifth behind the Bentleys.

For 1930 Chief Engineer Charles R. Greuter produced a cylinder head with twin overhead camshafts and four valves per cylinder; two Stutz DV32s thus-developed ran at Le Mans, both retiring. Still the public thought of any sporting Stutz as a 'Bearcat' and in the Depression new Bearcat and Super Bearcat models were launched which regrettably failed to save this classic marque.

Alfa Romeo Tipo 8C-2300
1933, Italy

Of all vintage and post-vintage sports-car manufacturers, perhaps Alfa Romeo of Milan have the finest reputation. Their products are the most sought-after and most valuable today. ALFA was established in 1910 as the Anonima Lombarda Fabbrica Automobili by Cavaliere Ugo Stella, who had formerly controlled the Italian branch of the French Darracq concern. The early ALFA cars were designed by Ing. Giuseppe Merosi, and in 1915 the company was taken over by an industrialist named Nicola Romeo. After the Armistice the cars were marketed as Alfa Romeos. Despite incredibly modest production levels Alfa Romeo were very interested in competition, starting in 1914 with an unsuccessful Grand Prix car. This interest flourished during the twenties; in 1924–25 the Alfa Romeo P2 Grand Prix cars dominated the sport and Alfa became World Champion Constructor.

Vittorio Jano, ex-Fiat, became Technical Head in place of Merosi in 1926 and his first touring and sports car designs gained instant respect – employing single- and twin-overhead-camshaft six-cylinder engines in 1500 and 1750cc forms. When supercharged these

cars dominated the major sports-racing events of 1928–30 with the exception of Le Mans, and 'the seventeen-fifty' Alfa became recognized as a great classic design. From 1931 to 1934 victory at Le Mans fell to Jano's enlargement of the 1750 theme – this model being the immortal 8C-2300 with straight-eight engine arranged in two in-line blocks of four cylinders divided by a central drive for the twin overhead camshafts.

With 2336cc capacity, a minimum of 130bhp at 4900rpm and a racing norm of 178bhp, the 8C-2300s were available in chassis lengths of 10ft 2in (the Le Mans model) or 9ft (Mille Miglia), and engines were occasionally taken out to 2.4 or even 2.6 litres. While a top speed of 105–110mph was standard, the very best Mille Miglia two-seater could achieve 125mph, a tremendous velocity for the time. In 1933 8C-2300s were placed 1-2-3 at Le Mans during their four-year domination of that prestigious event. But the model was expensive to produce, and only 188 or so were made – many of which happily survive today.

MG K3 Magnette
1933, Great Britain

Putting his back into the job Eddie Hall urges on his MG K3 Magnette on the Isle of Man in the early thirties.

MG is possibly the most famous of all sports-car marques as far as the general public is concerned, the initials being taken from Morris Garages, the company in Oxford from which William Morris (later Lord Nuffield) developed his industrial empire. The Garages were managed by Cecil Kimber and when, in 1920, William Morris's manufacturing company discontinued production of its own sporting version of the Morris Cowley, it was the Garages who began experimenting with different bodies and engine-tuning on Morris rolling chassis.

In 1924 Kimber produced a version of the 1.8-litre Morris Oxford which he fitted with a mildly tuned engine, an attractive aluminium body and up-rated suspension. By 1927 this MG was called the 14/40hp in honour of its improved engine output compared to the standard Morris 14/28. In 1928 Morris introduced the 2½-litre six-cylinder overhead-camshaft 'Six' and Kimber developed this with redesigned block and cylinder head to power his own MG 18/80hp. This model was further modified in 1930 with the fitting of a four-speed gearbox and stiffened chassis frame to form the 18/80 Mark II.

Meanwhile the Morris Minor-based 847cc MG Midget had made its mark. This M-Type MG was raced widely from 1930. The Abingdon-based company became synonymous with sports-car competition, and its products in both works team and private hands were hugely successful.

Kimber turned his attention to the 1930 Wolseley Hornet small six-cylinder and developed it into the MG F-Type Magna. This was offered in sports and touring versions with the 1271cc engine; from the Magna there was developed in 1932 the K1 Magnette saloon, followed rapidly by the K2 two-seater, and then the supercharged competition K3 Magnette 'racer'.

This remarkable 1086cc 140bhp sports-racing car won its class in the 1933 Mille Miglia and was driven to overall victory in the year's RAC Tourist Trophy at Ards by the Italian ace Tazio Nuvolari. K3s became universally respected as potent competition cars and excellent high-speed roadsters. Many were converted into true single-seater racing cars and the originals which survive today are highly prized and very valuable indeed.

Aston Martin 1½-litre Mk II
1935, Great Britain

Lionel Martin and Robert Bamford built their prototype car in 1914, deriving its name from Martin's and that of the Aston Clinton hillclimb venue. It used a 1.4-litre side-valve Coventry-Simplex engine mounted in an Isotta-Fraschini voiturette chassis; production commenced in 1922 and 60 or so of these cars and their immediate derivatives were built until 1925, many achieving considerable competition success.

The company was re-formed after 1925 and an overhead-camshaft 1½-litre model was designed by A. C. Bertelli, was tested in an Enfield-Allday racing-chassis frame, and entered production at Feltham, Middlesex, in 1927. The car's bodies were designed by Bertelli's brother Enrico and by 1929 the models were well-established. In 1931 a brief marketing link was forged with Frazer Nash and in 1933 the company came under the financial control and direction of R. G. Sutherland.

Bertelli and his partner W. S. Renwick had introduced their 'International' model in 1930, so called because it was equipped for road racing under International rules 'anywhere in the world'. The car employed dry-sump lubrication as standard and a close-coupled two/four seat body. 'Internationals' were made on chassis of two wheelbase-lengths, one 8 ft 6 in and the other 10 ft, and sports, saloon, tourer and coupé bodies were all adopted. In 1931 Astons had come second in their class in the Brooklands Double-12 Hour race and in 1931–32 won the Biennial Cup at Le Mans. In 1933 a Le Mans Replica model was catalogued using unit construction of engine and gearbox for the first time.

In 1934 a long chassis appeared carrying full four-seat tourer, coupé and saloon bodies, and in 1935 the Mark II emerged, identified by its chromed radiator grille and featuring a modified engine, still of 1495 cc but with improved crankshaft and valve-gear design, and giving 73 bhp. When the marque won the TT team prize in 1934 the stage was set for a super sports model named the Ulster in 1935. Offering 80 bhp at 5250 rpm and with a top speed of 102 mph, this was a true sports car which did much to confirm Aston Martin's ever-growing reputation.

1936 1½-litre Aston Martin Mk II low-chassis model in the JCC Brooklands Meeting of March 25, 1939.

Fiat Ballila
1935, Italy

The colossal Fiat company derives its name from the initials of its full title, Fabbrica Italiana Automobili Torino. It was founded in Turin in 1899 by Giovanni Agnelli, di Bricherasio and the Count Carlo Biscaretti di Ruffia. Fiat went racing widely until the mid-twenties while building a wide range of production vehicles of all types. In 1932 the advanced small Fiat was introduced as the Tipo 508 Balilla, with a short-stroke, four-cylinder engine. This three-main-bearing unit had a bore and stroke of 65 mm and 75 mm respectively – 995 cc. Essentially the Balilla, which had hydraulic brakes, was a modest little touring car, but sports versions accounted for about 1000 of the total 113,000 produced and they gave a good account of themselves in up-to-1100 cc-class sports-car racing.

The sports Balilla engine used pushrod overhead valves and delivered about 36 bhp; it was installed in a sketchily bodied vehicle whose weight was little more than 1340 lb. Performance was actually on a par with the far more august Lancia Aprilia, and the little Tipo 508S was virtually the only small Continental sports car in opposition to the British-built babies. It sold quite well and raced in many countries of Europe. The 1933 Mille Miglia saw special Balillas running with prototype overhead-valve heads and four-speed gearboxes made by the Siata tuning firm, before the overhead-valve engines came as standard to the production models in 1934.

Two types of Balilla sports car were built, sharing the same engine. One was the Spider Normale with flowing wings and the other the Spider Corso with cycle mudguards. Fiat also produced a Berlinetta Aerodinamica, a futuristic little fastback coupé. English-marketed Balillas had home-grown bodies with pronounced tail fins and the cars did very well indeed in rallies. In France Amédée Gordini's tuning company made its name with the French-built version known as the Simca.

Frazer Nash
1935, Great Britain

When Captain Archie Frazer-Nash left GN in around 1924 he tried building conventional family touring cars with shaft drive, but his sporting instincts triumphed and the Frazer Nash car (without the hyphen, notice) reverted to type. His prototype used GN-like dog-clutch gearchange with separate chains driving each of the three forward speeds, a solid rear axle, high-ratio steering and virtually solid leaf-spring suspension. The original Plus-Power engine was replaced by a side-valve water-cooled four-cylinder Anzani of $1\frac{1}{2}$-litres capacity, giving about 40 bhp. The Frazer Nash in this form attracted widespread popularity.

Such changes as there were centred mainly upon the power units adopted; an overhead-valve Meadows engine with 50 bhp and overhead valves replaced the Anzani from 1929, and was allied to four-speed transmission. The 'Nash was fast and nimble and could outcorner virtually anything on the open road, retaining this competitive edge far into the thirties. The Meadows-engined four-speed 'Boulogne' model of the early thirties could lap Brooklands quicker in third gear than in top – at around 80 mph. From 1934 the com-

Italy's much-loved little Fiat Ballila won fans throughout the world for its pert good looks and surprising performance.

pany's own engine (designed by Albert Gough and known by his name) was adopted; this unit displaced 1496cc and used a single overhead camshaft to produce 60bhp. Only 26 Gough-engined models left the Isleworth factory, between 1934 and 1938, and its bugs were never properly ironed out. In that same period a smoother six-cylinder Blackburne engine of 1657cc with twin overhead camshafts was used but only 27 of these cars were built. Cozette and Centric superchargers

were used on some Meadows- and Gough-engined 'Nashes, all these cars being built very much to customer specification.

Body changes had included the adoption of lower lines minus running boards in 1928, and of downswept chassis in 1934; the most popular style was the 'TT Replica' two-seater. Production of all Frazer Nash cars from 1923 onwards was only 348 units, and from 1934 AFN Ltd – controlled by the Aldington family – became BMW importer for the UK. Few 'Nashes were built postwar and today AFN are British Porsche importers.

Lagonda M45
1935, Great Britain

The Lagonda company was founded in Staines, Middlesex, by Wilbur Gunn – an American from Springfield, Ohio. He had come to England in 1897 and the following year completed his first air-cooled motor-cycle in a greenhouse at Staines.

After one of his motor-cycles had won the 1905 London-Edinburgh Trial, Gunn was encouraged to build a 20hp four-cylinder four-wheeled car, which he announced in 1907. In 1909 a Lagonda light car was introduced which survived in modified form into the mid-twenties.

In 1925 Arthur Davidson designed a 1954cc ohv sporting engine for Lagonda. From this 14/60 was developed the two-litre Speed Model for 1928, when the company's

parallel 2½-litre six-cylinder was enlarged to three litres.

Unfortunately Lagondas had the reputation for being underpowered and overweight. At the 1933 London Motor Show the 1104cc Rapier with twin overhead camshafts was introduced alongside the 4½-litre Meadows-engined M45. Now Lagonda had genuinely high performance models in their catalogue, and the racing M45R won Le Mans. Unfortunately the company was in trouble, being saved by businessman Alan Good who appointed W. O. Bentley as Chief Engineer. He produced the LG45 luxury model using the M45R engine and chassis, the LG6 of 1938 and the V12 model – considered to be Bentley's finest design.

Squire
1935, Great Britain

Adrian Squire was a gifted British enthusiast who had a vision of a $1\frac{1}{2}$-litre sports car built to the highest standards of design and execution, virtually regardless of cost. This was – of course – a recipe for financial disaster, but he established his company at Henley-on-Thames in 1934 and it survived for two years.

Squire himself had produced his own car catalogue when he was still a 16-year-old schoolboy; he was only 24 when his sports-car project appeared in the metal. He bought a $1\frac{1}{2}$-litre twin-overhead-camshaft four-cylinder engine from Anzani and modified it to his own requirements, then coupled to it a Roots supercharger to boost output to 110 bhp. The power unit was mated to a Wilson pre-selector gearbox, in which the driver merely flicked an indicator lever from gear to gear

before he required actual engagement, this being effected at the proper moment simply by dipping the clutch. These gearboxes were popular at the time, featuring in the MG K3s and the new ERA voiturettes. Squire developed his own hydraulic brake design using huge drums which filled the road wheels, and they were said to be so powerful that an emergency stop could in some cases shatter the front springs.

Vanden Plas produced a beautiful body for the car but beauty cost a great deal of money: the first Squire was priced at £1220, more than a $4\frac{1}{2}$-litre Lagonda and almost as much as a Bugatti Type 55. Squire had to face

British beauty – and an idealist's dream, Adrian Squire's craftsman-built 'special' was a commercial failure.

sobre reality and mount less attractive and more spartan bodies on later chassis, slashing his price to only £695, but hardly any customers came forward and the idealist's dream began rapidly to fade. Only seven cars were made and most of those were sold to personal friends of the constructor. In an attempt to gain publicity through racing, a single-seater was constructed but it proved very unreliable and did more to tarnish the image than gild it.

The company was liquidated in July 1936, the name, parts and goodwill being purchased by Val Zethrin, under whose control three final cars were assembled. The Squire was a beautiful little car but an excellent example of sports-car enthusiasm untempered by cold financial realism.

Delahaye 135 'Competition'
1936, France

The French company Delahaye was primarily a constructor of heavy commercial vehicles; virtually as a sideline, Delahaye built a range of very staid and dull touring cars from 1.5 to 2.8 litres in capacity. In 1935 this company saved Delage, who had declined from their great days of Grand Prix dominance in 1926–27 but still manufactured some of the world's most exciting and striking luxury high-performance cars.

After Delahaye had absorbed Delage its management smiled upon sports-car development. In 1934 Delahaye had introduced their Superluxe model, employing a 3.2-litre six-cylinder overhead-valve engine based on a truck design. Within the year Delahaye had produced two sizes of engine, not only the 110 bhp 3257 cc Coupe des Alpes but also the 120 bhp 3557 cc Type 135. The later engine in Competition form developed 160 bhp and the neat and prettily-bodied sports-racing car it powered was capable of 115 mph.

Delahaye used a Cotal electric gearbox which was delightfully quick and easy to use.

Gearchanges were by means of a tiny inch-long electrical switch operating within a conventional 'H'-pattern gate on the dashboard. The driver selected gears by flipping this switch to the required part of the gate, a large lever on the floor being pushed forward for forward drive or rearward for reverse; the car had four speeds in reverse as well as forward, so was theoretically capable of 115 mph tail-first. . . Latter-day private owner Rob Walker attempted this feat one day, and overturned his car!

Delahaye 135 Competitions were placed fifth at Le Mans in 1935; 2-3-4-5 in the 1936 French Grand Prix run for sports cars; second at Le Mans in 1937; and 1-3-4 at Le Mans in 1938.

Early in 1937 the French company introduced a 4½-litre V12 model whose 238 bhp engine shared the internal dimensions of Bentley's Lagonda V12; it doubled as a Grand Prix and sports-racing-car power unit – a Delahaye V12 two-seater coming fourth in the 1938 Mille Miglia.

HRG 1½-litre
1936, Great Britain

The famous 'Hurg' was the brainchild of H. R. Godfrey, who had formerly been responsible for the GN Cyclecars in partnership with Archie Frazer-Nash. Godfrey had been running his own business since this partnership dissolved in 1923, and in 1935 he developed his new car in collaboration with E. A. Halford and Guy A. Robins, choosing the title from a combination of their initials– *H*alford-*R*obins-*G*odfrey. HRG Engineering was based at Tolworth, near Kingston-upon-Thames, in Surrey.

The HRG was powered by a 1½-litre four-cylinder Meadows 4ED engine, which developed 60 bhp at 4500 rpm and was installed in a sketchy sporting frame with light-alloy two-seat bodywork. Suspension was by quarter-elliptic leaf springs at the front and semi-elliptics at the rear. In general form the car was very reminiscent of Frazer Nash practice but was lighter, had conventional transmission, could achieve 83 mph and was relatively inexpensive at only £395.

In 1939 the faithful Meadows engine was replaced by a 1½-litre overhead-camshaft Singer unit and HRG also offered a little 1100 cc sister car using the Singer Nine engine. HRG modified the engines consider-

ably, adopting stronger valve-springs, high-lift cam profiles and free-flow induction and exhaust manifolding; in competitions the little cars shone particularly brightly in off-road Trials, since the crew's weight was concentrated well over the back axle, aiding traction immensely. HRG cars were also widely raced and rallied; 1½-litre models even tackled the Le Mans 24-Hours classic in the years 1937–39; in 1938 they finished second in their class, and in 1939 they actually won their class.

Only 36 cars had been built when war broke out in September 1939. Postwar HRGs appeared little changed from immediate prewar trim, and they went on to even greater success in rallies, trials and minor racing events. HRG ceased car production in 1955 and the general engineering concern closed down finally in 1966. No more than 240 HRGs of all types were ever made.

'Hurg' on home ground: a 1937/8 1½-litre HRG in the Lawrence Cup Trial.

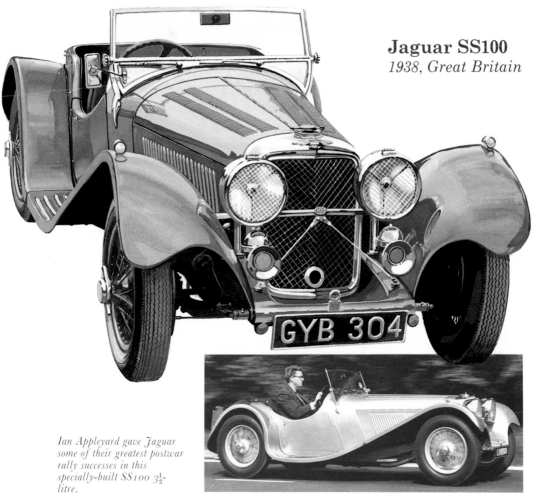

Jaguar SS100
1938, Great Britain

Ian Appleyard gave Jaguar some of their greatest postwar rally successes in this specially-built SS100 3½-litre.

The Swallow coachbuilding company, owned and run by William Lyons, first made its name with aerodynamic motor-cycle sidecars. It then progressed to a very attractive series of special car bodies. The logical sequel to the special body programme was the production of a car, and in 1931 the Coventry works indeed turned out a car using proprietary mechanical components.

This 'SS1' was powered by an untuned six-cylinder Standard 16 engine of 2054 cc mounted in an all-new underslung chassis frame built to Lyons's order by Standard. All this was clad in an exciting close-coupled coupé body, with very long bonnet and distinctly rakish, sporty lines. The price was a mere £310 for a car which looked incredibly exotic for that time. A baby sister model, known as the 'SS2' and using the four-cylinder Standard Little Nine engine, was also available. In 1933 a four-seat SS1 open tourer version was introduced and a team of these cars contested the

Alpine Trial. In March 1935 the SS90 two-seater sports made its debut and engineers William Heynes and Harry Weslake developed for it an overhead-valve cylinder head with twin carburettors which raised the Standard 2.6-litre engine's power output from 84 to 104 bhp.

For 1936 a new range of four-door saloons was introduced, known as the 'SS Jaguar', together with a new 2.6-litre two-seater, known as the 'SS100'. The SS100 was claimed to be capable of 100 mph and was wide and low, with flared front wings and a folding windscreen. With its humble pushrod engine of saloon car derivation, it was regarded with disdain by many enthusiasts as a showy 'special'. But for 1938 the SS100 was offered with a full 3½-litre engine delivering 125 bhp, and was now genuinely capable of 100 mph on any worthwhile stretch of straight road. These cars did very well in mid-level competition in Britain and Europe and laid the basis of the Jaguar sports-car activities which mushroomed postwar.

BMW 328
1937, Germany

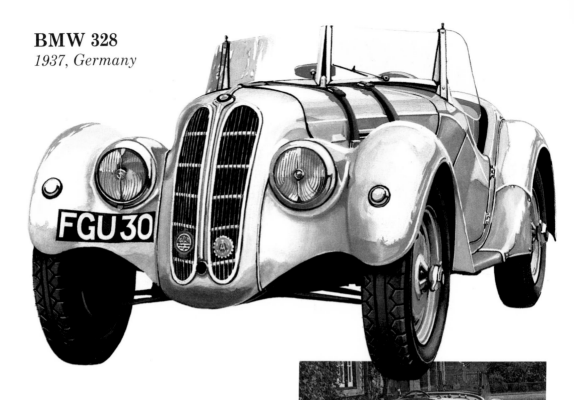

Early in their career, the Bayerische Motoren Werke built Austin Sevens under licence in Germany, and in 1930 they released a sports version known as the Dixi-Ihle. This was BMW's first sports model, and carried the sloped-back radiator grille which was to become familiar. BMW's own touring cars developed through better-handling and more powerful designs as the thirties progressed, until in 1934 a sports version of the Type 315 1490 cc six-cylinder was released, clad in a pretty two-seat body with spatted rear wheels. With three carburettors this model produced around 40 bhp and was good for 78 mph, and from it BMW developed the Type 319/1 1911 cc 'six' with 55 bhp and 90 mph maximum.

The six-cylinder engine proved eminently suitable for modification, tuning and enlargement and the BMW Type 326 four-door saloon used it in 1971 cc form. In the BMW 328 sports car, introduced in 1937, this enlarged 1971 cc engine was mated to a tubular Type 319/1 chassis frame, and a modified cylinder head was adopted in which a hemispherical combustion chamber for each cylinder housed inclined valves operated via cross-pushrods from a single overhead camshaft. The power unit was thus endowed with the performance characteristics of a true twin-overhead-camshaft engine without

The sleekly flared tail of the BMW sports car raised much comment at the time; note the disc-type spare wheel and massive fuel-filler neck.

the difficulties of building a twin-cam down to a realistic production price.

Fritz Fiedler was the designer responsible for the 328 and its predecessors, and his six-cylinder engine was renowned at the time for performing 'with a crisp suddenness that put it in the same class as the best overhead-camshaft engines'. It was also a very reliable unit which its post-war adoptive parents exploited fully. The BMW 328 chassis meanwhile featured precise rack-and-pinion steering; the live rear axle was suspended on semi-elliptic leaf springs, and the independent front suspension was by transverse leaf and wishbones. The result was that the car set standards of roadholding, cornering and

driving precision which had seldom been known before, certainly never in Germany.

Of more significance worldwide was the way the 328 pioneered weight-reduction and streamlining in a genuine production sports car. The car was able to produce exuberant performance from a basically humble specification, and sell at a price most could afford. Few enthusiasts, it has been said, were ever more justifiably fanatical than those who experienced the 328 in its heyday–a powerful, controllable and versatile design which has proved ageless.

At Le Mans in 1939 a BMW 328 took second place in the Index competition, and in 1940 special-bodied 328s placed first and third in

Tony Hutchings shone in sixties VSCC events with his 328. Here at Oulton Park in the rain in 1966 he heads an ERA.

the confined Mille Miglia road race in northern–and still neutral–Italy. Indeed, BMW sports cars were raced widely throughout Europe and in Britain, but their career was interrupted by World War II. After the cessation of hostilities in 1945 BMW's plants were split between the East and West German zones but BMW expertise reappeared in the Veritas, AFM and EMW sports-racing and Formula 2 cars, and in the British Bristols.

BMW 328 showing off its sleek lines on the starting grid for a VSCC race at Silverstone in the seventies.

Cisitalia 'Farina' Coupé

1947, France

Piero Dusio was an Italian industrialist, sometime racing driver and car enthusiast, with the ambition of recreating Italy's pre-war motoring dominance in the postwar years. He envisaged a motor-racing circus of identical low-price racing cars, based on Fiat parts, travelling the world and showing a spectacle-starved public the pick of the greatest racing drivers battling against one another on even terms. He employed Ing. Dante Giacosa to design his Cisitalia D46 racing cars with Fiat 1100cc pushrod overhead-valve engines in advanced space-frame chassis, and before an International Formula 2 class was established in Europe postwar, the Cisitalia circus did very well. Over 50 of these tiny 800lb, 65bhp racing cars were built.

Dusio then turned his attention to greater things. The Fiat engine promised much more as the basis of a production sports car, and if he was going to build a sports car Dusio wanted the best possible body mounted on it.

The chassis for the Cisitalia sports car was derived from that of the little D46 *vetturetta*, formed as a multi-tubular spaceframe on aircraft lines. Pinin Farina produced the enveloping bodyshell without the separate wings and running boards conventional pre-war, and the result was a profoundly influential Grand Touring and sports car which set the trend of Italian high-performance-car coachwork design which remains with us to this day. The combination of low weight and low aerodynamic drag from such a clean bodyshell enabled unheard-of performance to be extracted from that humble Fiat engine, Cisitalia's 50bhp Special Sport achieving 100mph and the 60bhp Mille Miglia screaming towards 120mph and beyond.

The 1947 Cisitalia's styling features were copied on both sides of the Atlantic; but by 1948 Dusio's immense investments in his Porsche-designed Grand Prix car and other business miscalculations led to Cisitalia's collapse and Dusio's own departure for Argentina.

MG TC

1948, Great Britain

In 1937 MG at Abingdon had adopted an engine developed from the Morris Ten-Four tourer, this being a 1292cc pushrod overhead-valve unit with little really to recommend it. It was fitted in what became known as the TA model; in 1939 the TB replaced it, using a new 1250cc engine which was to prove highly successful after World War II.

In November 1945 MG introduced their TC model, retaining the 1250cc 55bhp engine, but in a wider body with a number of minor specification improvements. Top speed of the TC was quoted as 78mph and with its separate flared wings, its running boards and separate headlamps it looked everything that a sports car – at that time – should.

The TC took the British sports-car tradition into the American export market with immense success. Its good handling compensated for a poor aerodynamic shape and relatively low power it ran out of steam towards 80mph.

Known also as the Midget, following the long MG tradition with that name, the TC had no peer for several years in the late forties. If one happened to be a sports-car enthusiast, one had to have a TC – it was the thing to do, and many aspiring racing and rally drivers on both sides of the Atlantic cut their teeth on TCs.

In January 1950 the MG TC was replaced by the TD, which offered coil-spring independent front suspension; wire wheels were replaced by discs, front and rear bumpers were standardized and again the body was widened to give a little extra cockpit room and comfort. The TD continued the TC's success despite cries of disgust from enthusiasts for the 'hair-shirt sports-car image'. In 1953 the TD was replaced by the TF model, which had its radiator raked back, a sloped slab tank at the rear and lamps fared into its wings. Extra power was available in the TF 1500 but

against the envelope-bodied aerodynamic cars from Austin-Healey and Triumph this was too little, too late. The brick-like MGs had had their day.

Veritas Saturn
1949, Germany

When peace settled over Europe in 1945 the landscape in general and industry in particular had been sorely ravaged. German factories were flattened and buried under heaps of charred rubble. Yet within a year enthusiasts were beginning to organize events for surviving touring and sporting cars—mostly hillclimbs. The BMW 328 was a popular weapon at this time and when some small establishments began building new cars, the old BMWs were a popular source of parts.

The best-known of all these postwar German products was Ernst Loof's Veritas built from 1948 to 1949 in Messkirch, from 1949 to 1950 in Rastatt and until 1953 at the Nürburgring circuit. Loof took the 1971cc BMW 328 six-cylinder engine with which he had been involved pre-war and installed it in a tubular frame clad in aluminium coachwork of very aerodynamic open-cockpit sports-racing-car design. This competition Comet model had a 140bhp engine and was good for 135mph,

while two more modest versions were also marketed, the Scorpion convertible and the Saturn fixed-head coupé.

In 1950 Veritas adopted a new single-overhead-camshaft 1988cc engine built for the company by Heinkel, of aviation fame, and this engine was also offered in numerous tune-states, from 100 to 140bhp. Five-speed transmissions were available with column gearchange on the coupés and a remote floor-shift in the competition models.

Between 1948 and 1950, when German enthusiasts were still barred from International competition outside their own frontiers, Veritas cars were entered in all manner of minor German sprints and races. They proved extremely successful at circuits such as the revived Nürburgring, Hockenheimring and Solitude, and also did well on the classical hillclimb courses as at Rossfeld and Freiburg.

The flowing curves of the XK120, one of William Lyons's classic creations. Demand surpassed all expectations.

Jaguar XK120
1950, Great Britain

In 1946 William Lyons's company in Coventry recommenced production of its SS Jaguar models, which continued to offer incredibly up-market looks and performance for very low prices. At the Brussels Salon in 1948 a streamlined Belgian bodyshell was shown on a pre-war SS100 chassis, and later that same year the London Motor Show was dominated by the appearance of the very latest, XK-series Jaguars. Two models were released, one the XK100 with a four-cylinder two-litre engine, while the sister XK120 used a six-cylinder, 3.4-litre engine. This seven-main-bearing design, with twin overhead camshafts, delivered 160 bhp at 5200 rpm from its 3442 cc. Front suspension was independent by

◄*In 1949 Jaguar test driver Len 'Soapy' Sutton drove this carefully prepared XK120 roadster – theoretically in standard mechanical trim – to average 132 mph on Belgium's Jabbeke Highway near Ostend.*

►*Another record version of the XK120, this time with bubble canopy enclosing the cockpit and 170 mph at Jabbeke!*

wishbones and torsion bars, and the Lyons-styled bodyshell was a graceful and attractive study in flowing lines with enclosing fenders and spatted rear wheels.

Demand for the larger-engined model was so great that the XK100 never entered production. The XK120 took the sports-car world by storm. Lyons had originally envisaged a production run of just 200 to sharpen the public's appetite for the XK-engined Mark VII Jaguar Saloon due in the coming year. Tooling for full production of the XK120 delayed progress, and the first export cars did not leave Britain's shores until the summer of 1949, and the first home market cars only became available in any quantity in 1951.

The XK120 name had been chosen to indicate that the car could achieve 120mph. In fact an independent road test by *The Motor* magazine recorded a maximum speed of 125 mph, and a works-prepared model with a streamlined undershield was officially observed to achieve 132.6mph on the Jabbeke Highway record strip near Ostend in Belgium. At Silverstone in 1949 XK120s finished 1-2-3 (incidentally, painted red, white and blue); later that year Ian Appleyard won the Alpine Rally in an XK120 and Stirling Moss the Tourist Trophy. In 1950 XKs raced at Le Mans, one running third for 21 hours.

Jaguar family, with the classically styled SS on the right, Appleyard's famous XK120 amidships and the D-Type on the left.

In 1951 a fixed-head-coupé version was introduced for those who wanted good looks and performance without the irritations of soft-top motoring, and in 1953 a drophead coupé added more civilization to the range.

In 1951 'Competition', or C-Type, versions of the XK120 were developed for Le Mans using bodies of revised aerodynamic form designed by the brilliant Malcolm Sayer, and an all-new tubular chassis frame. The C-Types won the 24-Hours, and came in 1-2-4 in the Tourist Trophy. Jaguar competition achievements were to include a total of five Le Mans victories during this decade.

In 1954 the XK120 was replaced by the XK140, which looked very similar but had an engine re-tuned to deliver 190bhp. In 1957 the XK150 coupés replaced the 140s, the D-Type competition-based XK-SS being intended to act as the open roadster model of the range. The omission was made good in 1958 by the release of the XK150S roadster, which used a 250bhp 3.8-litre version of the XK twin-cam six-cylinder engine and had disc brakes all round. It remained in production until superceded by the immortal E-Type in 1961.

Le Mans Talbot-Lago

1950, France

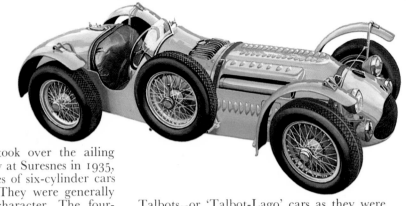

Major Antoine Lago took over the ailing French Talbot company at Suresnes in 1935, introducing a new series of six-cylinder cars with overhead valves. They were generally pleasant, if sobre in character. The four-litre 23CV model with seven-main-bearing crankshaft and in Lago Special trim cross-pushrod valve gear *à la* BMW delivered 165 bhp and would exceed 100 mph on any worthwhile straight. Similar cars were placed 1-2-3 in the 1937 French Grand Prix for sports cars at Montlhéry. For the 1938 39 Grand Prix Formula which catered for supercharged three-litre and unsupercharged 4½-litre racing engines, Lago authorized two lines of approach. One was a supercharged three-litre V16 engine designed by former Fiat and Sunbeam-Talbot-Darracq engineer Walter Becchia, and the second a more modest, unblown 4½-litre 'six' derived from existing power units. The V16 was rapidly shelved owing to the unavailability of sufficient capital before the war, while the unblown 4½ could not compete with the German might of that time.

After the war the situation was rather different, for against the supercharged 1½-litre Italian Grand Prix cars the 4½-litre Lago-

Talbots or 'Talbot-Lago' cars as they were actually lettered stood a better chance, particularly since they could run through a Grand Prix distance non-stop while the highly supercharged predominantly Italian opposition had to make at least one and sometimes two stops to take on extra fuel.

Louis Chiron and Louis Rosier both won Grand Prix races with these cars in the late-forties and in 1950 Rosier and his son shared their 'Lago Record' Grand Prix model in the Le Mans 24-Hour endurance classic, the car being rigged up with cycle-type wings and head- and tail-lamps for the occasion. This remarkable special out-ran all the opposition and survived the day-long grind with imperious reliability and ease, Rosier Sr driving 23½-hours and only allowing his son a brief 30-minute stint by way of relief. This was a sensational achievement for any true Grand Prix car, quite apart from being a remarkable personal feat of high-speed driving skill and endurance.

Healey Silverstone

1951, Great Britain

Before World War II, Donald Healey was Triumph's engineering director and a very successful rally driver. When the war ended in

Europe in May 1945, with ex-Alfa Romeo engineer A. C. Sampietro he set about design of a sports car to carry his own name. Their first product was offered as a well-streamlined four-seat roadster or a two-door saloon, using

a Riley 2.4-litre overhead-valve, four-cylinder engine. In 1946 the Healey proved itself Britain's fastest production saloon, achieving 104.7mph under test. Early Healeys such as this won their class in the 1947 and 1948 Alpine Trials, and won the Touring Car Class in the 1949 Mille Miglia.

The Healeys were, however, very expensive in their home market and for 1950 Donald Healey introduced his much lighter and simpler Silverstone sports model which, while no faster than the sobre-bodied saloon, was very reliable, inexpensive and much more fun. Many budding British and American racing drivers cut their competition teeth in Silverstone models, many of them actually on the former airfield racing circuit in Northamptonshire after which the model was named.

In December 1949, talks had begun between Healey and George W. Mason, President of the Nash-Kelvinator Corporation of America,

concerning the possibility of collaboration on a sports car. A prototype was run at Le Mans in 1950 which beat all American-engined opposition there. This experimental Nash-Healey finished fourth overall and in the autumn of 1950 Nash-Healeys made their production debut. Eventually Donald Healey's Warwick factory dropped the Silverstone and other models to concentrate upon Nash-Healey production for the US market – the Silverstone chassis being used virtually as was to accommodate the long-stroke six-cylinder Nash engine.

But in 1952 Healey displayed his prototype envelope-bodied Healey '100' at the Earls Court Motor Show in London. Austin were smitten with it and agreed to put it into volume production as the 'Austin-Healey', and so all other projects took second place; Austin-Healey had been born and was to dominate.

The Allard J2, a combination of British and American engineering, was as virile as it looked.

Allard J2
1952, Great Britain

Sidney Allard was an inveterate special-builder, and a sprint and hillclimb driver of considerable skill. He built his first Allard car in the mid-thirties using Ford engine and chassis, and Bugatti body and steering. His successful, mud-plugging Allards were much sought-after in trials and hillclimb circles before World War II. Immediately after the war Sid Allard returned to the hills with a fearsome device using a Steyr V8 air-cooled military engine and, eventually, four-wheel drive. In 1947 and 1948 Allard was among the top three drivers in the RAC British Hillclimb Championship and he won it in 1949.

He had formed his own Allard Motor Company in London in 1946 and introduced two fast touring cars, the models K and L, and began development of a smaller, lightweight competition car, powered by an American Mercury engine. In 1949 the Allard J2 was unveiled – an ugly, purposeful, virile competition and road-going sports car of undiluted savagery. Sid Allard intended it to carry low-price, economical and powerful American V8 power from Ford or Cadillac. With split-axle

independent front suspension and transverse leaf-spring rear end, the Allard-Cadillac became a much sought-after imported sports car in the USA.

Allard-Cadillacs scored in road races right across the USA. Enthusiasts such as Erwin Goldschmidt, Tom Cole, Fred Wacker and Tom Carstens drove and entered J2s with immense success. Goldschmidt's V8 engine developed just under 300bhp and his Allard accelerated from 0–60mph in under seven seconds, 0–100mph in under 14 seconds and could reach nearly 160mph in a fearless straight line, staggering figures for the time. Sid Allard took a J2 into third place in the 1950 Le Mans 24-Hours race. Gradually, more modern concepts overtook the tail-heavy design of the J2, bred from trials and hillclimb competition, and so Allards became more sophisticated. However, they never lost the win-or-bust image characteristic of those fierce, V8-engined J2s.

Porsche 356
1951, Germany

Old Dr Ferdinand Porsche of pre-war Löhner, Austro-Daimler, Steyr, Mercedes-Benz, Auto Union and Volkswagen design fame was interned by the French authorities at the end of World War II, while in Austria his son 'Ferry' established the Porsche Büro design office at Gmünd. There he built prototypes and the first handful of production models under the Porsche name, these being lightweight sporting cars based on VW mechanical parts.

In 1950 serious Porsche production commenced at Stuttgart-Zuffenhausen in Germany. The first model was known as the Type 356. It used a rear-mounted air-cooled VW engine of 1086cc mounted in the car's tail actually behind the rear axle line and delivering around 40bhp. The Porsche 356 series developed from this root ran virtually unchanged in basic shape until as recently as 1964, when the 2000GS model was running a 1996cc Porsche flat-four air-cooled engine which delivered an honest 130bhp with performance to match.

Porsche's early reputation was built rapidly on racing, sprinting, hillclimb and rallying success, not only in Europe but around the world. The factory entered cars at Le Mans as early as 1951 when they won the 1100cc class; in 1952 Porsches won the 1500cc class in the Mille Miglia, the 1100cc class again at Le Mans, and were 1-3-4 in the gruelling open-road race known as the Liège-Rome-Liège Rally.

The stubby little Porsches handled very well with suitable suspension tuning to overcome the inherent tail-wagging effect created by their rear-engine layout; and their light weight combined with adequately powerful engines gave them a very fine power-to-weight ratio which matched their high-speed cornering abilities. In addition Porsche's engineering skills were of the highest standard; the cars had reliability built into them, a tradition still evident today in the company's painstaking test and development programmes, and almost flawless attention to quality finish and fine detail.

The Porsche 356 in Coupé, Roadster and Cabriolet forms was very neat and pretty.

Aston Martin DB2
1952, Great Britain

The well-established but always precarious Aston Martin company underwent change of ownership (by no means the first) in 1947, with its acquisition by industrialist David Brown. Claude Hill, Aston's Chief Engineer, already had a new postwar design on the stocks when this management change took place and his car was introduced as the DB1, taking David Brown's initials.

The DB1 used a four-cylinder pushrod overhead-valve engine of 1970cc which developed around 90bhp. It had independent front suspension and was available both as a drophead coupé and as a sports tourer. In 1949 a 2580cc twin-overhead-camshaft six-cylinder Lagonda engine was mounted experimentally in a DB1 chassis frame and in the spring of 1950 this hybrid model entered production as the Aston Martin DB2, employing an all-enveloping two-door, two-seat coupé body. The engine was offered in standard form with a 6.5:1 compression ratio and 105bhp, and in tuned 'Vantage' trim with 8.16:1 compression and 125bhp.

The DB2 was a potent competition car with tremendous potential, and the works team campaigned the model very actively across Europe. In 1950 and 1951 the DB2s did well at Le Mans while never having the sheer power necessary to challenge Ferrari and Jaguar seriously, and a DB2 won its class in the 1951 Mille Miglia race around Italy.

In 1954 an enlarged version was introduced, known as the 'DB2/4' and incorporating two occasional seats in the back of the cabin for use by children or by the 'legless midgets' so beloved of contemporary motoring journalists.

Ex-Auto Union engineer Dr Robert Eberan von Eberhorst was retained by Brown to develop a true competition model for the company, and this emerged first as the DB3 employing a tubular chassis frame and open roadster bodywork which won the Goodwood Nine-Hours race in 1952. Late that year DB3s were fitted with 2912cc engines which then found their way into an improved DB2/4 capable of 125mph. In 1953 the curvaceous DB3S sports-racer was developed from the DB3 to become the centrepiece of the beautiful Aston Martin competition line.

Peter Collins brakes his works-entered Aston Martin DB3S on the Dundrod RAC TT course in Ulster, 1955.

Austin-Healey 100
1952, Great Britain

Austin fell for the envelope-bodied good looks of the 2.6-litre Austin-powered Healey sports roadster at the 1952 London Motor Show, and a mass-production agreement was quickly forged between the two companies. This was the first real indication of postwar interest in high-performance cars on the part of a really large British manufacturer, and the Austin-Healey carved itself tremendous markets at home and abroad—notably in America at the expense of the now dated-looking, separate-fendered MGs.

The simple 2.6-litre four-cylinder Austin engine delivered about 90 bhp at 4000 rpm and, with a simple box-section frame beneath that pretty body, and independent front suspension built from proprietary components, production was relatively inexpensive. Thanks to its good shape the Austin-Healey offered very lively acceleration up to a maximum of about 105 mph and in 1953 early long-distance record-breaking attempts in search of publicity yielded 123 mph over 12 hours, and then 103 mph over 30 hours running in what was claimed to be standard trim.

The Austin engine proved itself very responsive to competition tuning and Austin-Healeys excelled in amateur speed events of all kinds. The 100M was introduced in 1954 with 110 bhp engine and lightweight bodywork, and the 100S was offered 'for export only' with 132 bhp, disc brakes and much-modified cylinder head and camshaft.

In 1956 production of the four-cylinder Austin power unit was discontinued and so the first six-cylinder Austin-Healey appeared with a slightly reduced displacement but 12 extra horsepower. The Austin-Healey 100-6 had added smoothness and torque from the six-cylinder engine and acquired a beautiful exhaust note which was music to Healey enthusiasts' ears. Weight increased, unfortunately, from around $18\frac{1}{2}$ cwt to over a ton and performance was not noticeably improved by comparison with four-cylinder trim.

The effect of modern racing regulations upon road sports cars is often hideous—here a Healey 100 has suffered.

Pegaso Z102B
1952, Spain

In the late thirties, after Vittorio Jano had left to join Lancia, design responsibility at Alfa Romeo devolved upon a Spaniard named Wilfredo Ricart. He designed many extraordinarily complex and ambitious chassis and engines before the war years, which he spent with the company, finally returning to his native Spain in the late forties. There he became chief engineer of the ENASA Pegaso company which was built upon the remnants of the old Hispano-Suiza concern in Barcelona, and which was to be involved primarily with the construction of heavy lorries.

As a prestige exercise, Ricart convinced his board of directors that a very high-priced exotic sports car would prove immensely valuable to the company. At the same time its construction would give the company trainees proper pride in workmanship before they embarked on the fairly humdrum business of building trucks and buses.

Ricart was given the go-ahead, and in 1951 his new car created a sensation at the Paris Salon. The car used a four-cam V8 engine which was virtually a Grand Prix racing design with little concession to production economies or restrictions. This 2½-litre engine was capable of delivering 165 bhp at 6500 rpm in standard tune. It was mated to a five-speed gearbox in unit with the rear axle at the back of the car, and De Dion rear suspension coupled with coil-and-wishbone independent front suspension added still more to its Grand Prix character.

The car employed a simple platform chassis and upon this base the leading coachbuilders of the age were invited to weave their magic. Since there was no indigenous Spanish components industry to speak of, Pegaso had to build more of their own car than any similar manufacturer, even making their own brakes and bearings. Saoutchik of Paris and Carrozzeria Touring of Milan were the most popular Pegaso coachbuilders, and their products attracted astronomical prices for the time. But the cars handled and performed well and one competition version became briefly the World's fastest production car – being officially timed at 152 mph through the flying kilometre. Then Jaguar spoiled things by reaching 172 mph. The last Pegaso car was delivered in 1958.

The Spanish Pegaso was named after Pegasus, the flying horse, and had distinctly equine styling to match. Alternative bodies were happily available.

Triumph TR2
1953, Great Britain

Perhaps the Triumph TR range of inexpensive sports cars, economical to run, yet with undoubted high performance, reached its peak with the introduction of the muscular TR4 model in September 1962. By that time over 80,000 TR3 and TR3As had been produced and the new model, with its square-cut, chunky Italian styling by Michelotti, proved a worthy replacement.

It used the trusty Triumph four-cylinder engine in 2138cc form, developing 105 bhp gross at 4600 rpm, which was transmitted via a very pleasant-to-operate, four-speed-and-reverse, all-synchromesh gearbox. The independent front suspension with coil springs was retained from the model's immediate predecessor, the TR3A, along with the live rear axle on half-elliptic leaf-springs. The TR4 was based upon a slightly wider chassis frame than that used in the TR3 family, and proved very attractive upon its introduction, reasonably priced at £1095 in open form and £1146 as a closed two-seat coupé. A detachable 'Surrey top' proved an unusual innovation, the roof panel alone detaching to leave a fixed rear screen still in place. Wind-up side windows completed the cockpit protection.

The new model had a 0–50 mph acceleration time of just over seven seconds, which was quite brisk in those days; it could cover the standing-start quarter mile in 17.5 seconds, and had a top speed of about 110 mph.

In January 1965 the TR4A was announced, this being the first all-independently-suspended sports car in the TR range. It used the Triumph 2000 saloon-car independent rear suspension with trailing-arm and coil springs; with 104 bhp it was slightly heavier than the TR4 which it replaced, 40,300 TR4s having been produced. The TR4A was never quite a match for the TR4 either in a straight line or around corners, but it rode more comfortably and was more refined. Some 28,500 TR4As were built before the model's disappearance in August 1968, the fuel-injection TR5 and restyled TR6 continuing the tradition until the advent of the modern TR7 coupé in the seventies.

▲*Enthusiasts were quick to take the Triumph TRs into competition–here a TR2 is tackling the 1953 RAC Rally of Great Britain.*

◀*TR chase on another rally night stage, 1953...*

AC Ace
1954, Great Britain

The famous AutoCarrier company was founded by engineer John Weller in 1908, taking residence at Thames Ditton, Surrey three years later. In 1913 the company brought out a 10hp four-cylinder light car, and in 1919 Weller introduced what was to become his famous 1991 cc single-overhead-camshaft wet-liner six-cylinder AC engine. This entered production in 1922 and stayed in the catalogue until 1963; over the years development punched its original output of around 35 bhp up to more than 100 bhp. In the fifties this unit was to power the AC Ace shown here.

AC was under the direction of famous racing driver and entrepreneur Selwyn Francis Edge from 1921 to 1929 and cars were raced, sprinted and hillclimbed widely with great success. The company suffered in the Depression years and was acquired by the Hurlock family in 1930. In 1947 production recommenced after the war with a range of high-performance saloon and three-wheeled invalid cars, and the Petite 350cc motor-cycle-engined convertible. Then in 1953 the Hurlocks took up a twin-tube-chassis, all-independently suspended sports-car design by John Tojeiro, wearing a body modelled after that of the successful Ferrari 166 Barchetta sports-racing car. This was fitted with the famous AC six-cylinder engine and going into production as the AC Ace in 1954 it became a terrific success; a true 100 mph two-seat sports car in classical mould with the modern lines of a wheel-enclosing bodyshell. The Ace handled very well and achieved a long string of race successes in amateur events as well as proving itself a fine road-going sports car.

AC later adopted more powerful six-cylinder Bristol engines of 2 litres' and 2.2 litres' capacity and derived from the BMW 328; eventually they turned to the economy, reliability and adequate power of the 2.6-litre Dagenham Ford engine. Disc brakes became standard on the cars in 1960 and it was upon the pretty little Ace that Carroll Shelby based his Ford V8-engined conversion –the fearsome Shelby American Cobra.

Ted Whiteaway/Jack Turner drove this AC Ace home in an astonishing seventh place overall behind four Ferraris and the victorious Aston Martins at Le Mans in 1959.

Jaguar D-Type
1954, Great Britain

While over 50 C-Type Jaguars were manufactured in series from August 1952 to 1954 for sale to private owners with competition aspirations, the Coventry works team required a new, more aerodynamic, and lighter weapon for their own front-line competition against the might of Ferrari, Maserati, Lancia and Mercedes-Benz.

For 1954 the D-Type emerged, based on a stressed-skin monocoque central chassis nacelle built on aviation principles. In this the panels curving round to form the visible external body of the car were fixed permanently to internal bulkheads, thus forming the major load-bearing structural members of the frame without resort to separate tube or girder members. A front subframe accepted the independent front suspension while a live axle was retained at the rear. This was generally maintained throughout the D-Types' long competition career and in fact it limited their effectiveness to ultra-smooth high-speed circuits such as Le Mans, which Sir William Lyons rightly identified as Jaguar's primary target—the most prestigious sports-

car race in the world, victory in which would pay the biggest dividends in terms of sales.

Jaguar D-Type cars followed upon the C-Type's success; a D-Type was placed second at Le Mans in 1954, running a 3.4-litre engine against the 4.9-litre V12 engine of the winning Ferrari; D-Types won the classic endurance grind in 1955, 1956 and 1957—Jaguar thus equalling Bentley's record of five 24-Hour race victories at Le Mans in an overall period of seven years. D-Types also won the Sebring 12-Hours race in Florida, USA, in 1955 and at Watkins Glen, USA, in 1955–6–7. About 50 competition D-Types were built, and a road-equipped sister model, the XK-SS, was laid down for full series production at the Browns Lane works. Tragically the factory was destroyed by fire in February 1957 when only 16 of the 144 mph XK-SS models had been completed, and its production was abandoned after the works was rebuilt, Jaguar concentrating on development of the new monocoque-chassis E-Type instead.

Mike Hawthorn completes a miserable race in the rain at Le Mans with his D-Type Jaguar after being involved in the third-hour tragedy which killed over eighty spectators...

Closely related to its Grand Prix sister, the 300 SLR resorted to air braking!

Mercedes-Benz 300 SLR
1955, Germany

When the Daimler-Benz AG directors authorized an all-out Grand Prix racing programme for 1954, they added a sports-car project to run in parallel. The new car was to use a three-litre version of the 2.5-litre straight-eight fuel-injected Grand Prix engine. The Mercedes publicity people recalled the famous gull-wing-doored, Le Mans-winning 300SL coupés of 1952, and dubbed their new sports-racing model the 300SLR. To run a mere three-litre sports-racer against the 3.4s from Jaguar and the 4.0s from Ferrari seemed like folly but Mercedes were using a pure-bred racing engine, instead of a modified production model.

The startling 300SLRs' first race was the Italian Mille Miglia in March 1955, and Stirling Moss and his navigator, Denis Jenkinson, won at the stunning average of 97.95 mph over the 1000 miles on public roads. Tested after the race, their car's engine still delivered 296 bhp at 7400 rpm, at which speed it was geared to drive the car at 170 mph. Fangio's sister car, driven solo, was second. In May Fangio, Moss and Karl Kling were placed 1-2-4 in the Eifelrennen at Nürburgring, and at Le Mans a terrific 'Grand Prix' race raged furiously during the first two hours between the 300SLRs, Castellotti's Ferrari and Hawthorn's D-Type Jaguar. This was resolved tragically at the time of the first scheduled refuelling stops as veteran French driver 'Pierre Levegh' (Bouillon) crashed his 300SLR off the tail of Lance Macklin's Austin-Healey while passing between the pit row and the crowded grandstands and hurtled into the crowd, killing himself and over 80 spectators. Daimler-Benz withdrew their cars after leading until midnight.

Fangio and Moss finished 1-2 in the Swedish Grand Prix and Moss won the Tourist Trophy from an inspired Hawthorn in his Jaguar; other 300SLRs finished second and third once the D-Type had broken. Now for the Sports Car world title, and entries were made for the Sicilian Targa Florio in October. Moss and Peter Collins shared 300SLR/0004 and brought it home to victory despite two accidents en route. Other 300SLRs were placed second and fourth. Mercedes-Benz were double Champions of the World and retired from racing forthwith.

Gullwing showing why – the pet name for the road-going Mercedes-Benz 300SL Coupé was most descriptive.

Sunbeam Alpine
1955, Great Britain

Sunbeam developed from John Marston's tinplate and japanware company in Wolverhampton, Staffordshire, which had been making bicycles since 1887 and which built its first belt-drive prototype car in 1899. The first cars to enter production were the diamond-pattern four-wheel Sunbeam-Mabley voiturettes of 1901–04, which were claimed to be skid-proof. The company was reformed as the Sunbeam Motor Car Co. Ltd in 1905 and from 1909 enjoyed a period of great success in the forefront of international motor-racing competition, bursting with prestige and dynamism and building some very fine cars indeed. In 1920 Sunbeam amalgamated with Talbot and Darracq to form the Anglo-French S-T-D combine which was to collapse in 1935, whereupon the Sunbeam company was acquired by Rootes.

The Rootes Group revived the Sunbeam name after World War II and in 1953 it was given to the Alpine, a two-seat version of the 2.3-litre Sunbeam-Talbot 90, with its overhead-valve, four-cylinder engine. The Alpine won four coveted Coupes des Alpes in the Alpine Rally of 1953, and Stirling Moss won a Gold Cup and Sheila van Damm the Ladies' Cup in the Alpine Rally of 1954. The Alpine was a genuine 100mph car when properly tuned and was very attractive and handsome for its day, although very much a convertible touring car rather than a true sports roadster.

The model was discontinued in October 1955, but the Sunbeam Alpine name was revived in 1960 for a low-slung unit-construction sports roadster with 1494cc 78bhp engine which was handsome in a typically under-stated Rootes manner, and was good for a genuine 98mph. This model was a civilized and comfortable road tourer; it was too heavy for serious competition although the factory team campaigned lightened versions in the longer sports-car events such as Le Mans and Sebring. From this model the Sunbeam Tiger was later developed, with its American Ford V8 engine.

MGA
1956, Great Britain

As early as 1951 the MG technical team at Abingdon, headed by the brilliant Sydney Enever, realized that the company would head for disaster if Nuffield Group management insisted upon retaining in production the T series cars with their outdated, non-aerodynamic body shapes. For Le Mans in 1951 a prototype MG was constructed carrying a streamlined wheel-enclosing bodyshell on a TC chassis frame. This was intended as an experimental production prototype, and Enever decided it required a new chassis frame which indeed made it into an eminently saleable proposition, but the remote management controlling MG's destinies at this time did not recognize the new car's potential.

In 1952 the new Triumph and Austin-Healey sports cars appeared with their enveloping bodies, and hammered more nails into the coffin of the T-series MG. Finally the go-ahead was given for Enever's brainchild to enter production. It finally emerged in Sept-

ember 1955 as the svelte and beautiful MGA, after a team of three prototype cars had run with some success at Le Mans.

With a 68 bhp engine, the MGA matched the 98 mph maximum speed of a race-tuned 97 bhp MG TF with unstreamlined bodywork. The better aerodynamic shape of the MGA clearly paid tremendous dividends and using the 1489 cc four-cylinder engine shared by the ZA Magnette saloon the MGA was set fair for considerable commercial success. In fact its production run in seven years was to exceed 100,000.

A rather exotic twin-overhead-camshaft engine was also developed for the MGA, but this version was produced in relatively very modest numbers, and was not to prove very popular, although effective in competition use. A Twin-Cam MGA was the first MG to have front disc brakes as standard, and in 1960 discs appeared in the 1588 cc MGA 1600, which replaced the smaller-engined original model. Both two-seat open roadster and fixed-head coupé models were available, the MGA combining beautifully responsive and safe handling characteristics with considerable agility and speed.

The pretty MGA Hardtop in an unlikely setting—grass-track autocross at Taunton in the sixties.

Chevrolet Corvette
1956, United States

General Motors' first Corvette was thought of as nothing more than a glittering show car, all chromium plate and promises. Not even GM, it was said, could possibly market a special-bodied sporting device like that for under $4000. But Chevrolet knew better. The Detroit giant astounded the American enthusiast public by entering full production with the car and at last doing something, just a little, to fend off the imported European sports-car threat.

The first Corvette appeared at the end of 1953 using a stock six-cylinder 3.7-litre side-valve workhorse engine tuned to deliver 160 bhp. The two-seat roadster bodyshell was the world's first in relatively large production to employ glass-reinforced polyester tech-niques; it was a 'glass-fibre' moulding. The Corvette offered the American market adequate performance combined with reasonably flat cornering—despite the softness of the suspension, which made for a much more comfortable and willowy ride than that offered by the hard-sprung Europeans, such as the MGs. Of the European cars, it was said that if one drove over a silver dollar lying in the road, one could tell whether it was heads or tails. Although their engine displacement was actually modest compared with some of the imports, independent road test reports soon confirmed that the earliest Corvettes were quick enough, easy to drive without tiring out their driver, and furthermore that they could out-drag Jaguars from the traffic lights while being able to out-corner any other American car on the open highway.

The first hand-made production Corvette leaves the Flint (Michigan) production line, June 30, 1953.

The completely restyled 1958 Hardtop model with V8 engine and deeply scalloped sides.

Corvette '73 featured the later-style body with integral urethane-covered bumper up front.

▲ *Moody public relations and advertising photography does its best for the 1956 Chevy Corvette, which was actually a much larger motor-car than it appears to be from this angle.*

◄ *When GM adopted glass-reinforced-plastic body construction for the Chevrolet Corvette it created a sensation. Here this 1953 release photograph shows the major mouldings pre-assembly.*

Even a pussyfoot driver could feel content and safe at 108 mph along the 'straightaways' in his plastic-bodied special, and some Corvettes just happened to go together right and they were good for 110 mph at least. Where the Corvette lost marks was under braking, for hard driving in hilly country would fade out its drum brakes completely. The provision of Powerglide automatic transmission as standard in the early cars disappointed many would be owners but as the type developed so its sporting essence was distilled and refined.

In 1956 a 4.3-litre overhead-valve V8 180 bhp engine was introduced in the Corvette line; by 1960 handling had been greatly improved and a fuel-injected 290 bhp engine option was available.

For 1963 the styling was completely revised and the redesigned Corvette Stingray appeared with multi-curvature body and pointed nose with retractable podded headlamps, all powered by a 5.3-litre 360 bhp V8 engine. This machine proved immensely popular on the American market and appealed to one or two exhibitionists in Great Britain and Europe. In 1968 the model was again restyled with engine options of 5.3 litres and seven litres.

In the course of the fifties and sixties, the Corvette became America's best-loved indigenous sporting car, and one which in its many variations has an immense following today in Corvette Clubs throughout America.

Maserati 300S
1956, Italy

The Maserati brothers of Bologna built their company's reputation on motor-racing achievement through the thirties. After World War II a 1488cc six-cylinder sports model known as the A6-1500 was introduced, wearing an enveloping body vaguely reminiscent of the 1940 Mille Miglia BMW 328, and it raced without proper development in 1947–48 while the Orsi-owned Maserati company concentrated upon single-seater racing-car production. A parallel road-going model was produced, bodied usually by Pinin Farina, and there was also the slender-bodied cycle-wing 'A6GCS' 1978cc six-cylinder which was produced in two series into 1955.

The first of the true all-enveloping bodied sports-racing Maseratis was released in the 1955 Nürburgring 500km race as the four-cylinder 1484cc 140bhp '150S' model. It won the race, driven by Jean Behra. The 150S proved very popular among amateur drivers as it was relatively inexpensive to buy and to operate without factory assistance. It appears that about 27 of these cars were produced between January 1955 and March 1957.

For 1956 the *Tipo* 52 Maserati '200S' was introduced using a 92mm bore × 75mm stroke 1993cc version of the four-cylinder engine with twin overhead camshafts delivering 186bhp at 7500rpm. This 150mph motor car proved very successful and was popular again with amateur drivers, particularly in the USA. Production ran from April 1956 to July 1958 and totalled probably 33 cars, wearing all manner of sports-racing roadster bodies almost invariably of beautiful appearance.

Late in 1958 a 96mm × 86mm, 2489cc four-cylinder model was released as the Maserati 250S with 236bhp at 7000rpm and a top speed of some 162mph using the lightweight chassis of the smaller-engined cars. Four of these were built. Meanwhile a six-cylinder 2991cc 300S with 280bhp had been produced from 1955 to 1958, no less than 30 of these purebred racers being built, while there were also 350S (325bhp–four built) and 450S (400bhp V8–10-11 built) sports-racing cars from the factory in Viale Ciro Menotti, Modena.

Ferrari 250 Testa Rossa
1958, Italy

Enzo Ferrari was in control of Alfa Romeo's motor racing on a private basis from 1933 to 1937; after World War II his own Ferrari company began production of an ever-growing range of competition and high-performance road-going cars which won innumerable race victories worldwide, and consequent international acclaim.

Ferrari dominated International sports-car racing for several years with a wide variety

1958 Ferrari 250 Testa Rossa

of cars, but none was more famous than their Testa Rossa ('Red-Head') models of the late fifties, which are now collectors' cars and much sought after. The first prototype 250 Testa Rossa appeared in the Nürburgring 1000 km race in May 1957, with a V12 three-litre engine with a single overhead camshaft per bank. It finished tenth. Later cars that year featured cut-away cheeks and the 'pontoon-fendered' body style. They had independent coil-and-wishbone front suspension with live rear axles on leaf springs; the engines, which won the type its name by their red crackle-finished cam-covers, delivered 300 bhp at 7200 rpm.

For 1958 De Dion rear axles were adopted and that May saw the pontoon-fender body-work replaced by more conventional styling. At Le Mans that year the very successful 250 'TR' Ferraris (which bore no relation whatsoever to the humble Triumph TRs) made up nine of the ten Maranello cars entered – the odd man out being a four-cylinder two-litre, also with red heads. For 1959 a much lighter Testa Rossa sports-racing car was devised with the driver on the right and the engines offset to the left to balance his weight. Whereas the Pininfarina bodywork had been made previously by Scaglietti, that company was now committed to Ferrari 'California' production work and Fantuzzi – formerly the Maserati bodybuilder – took over Ferrari's work on the competition cars with several external changes to the styling, including the provision of barred air-exit grilles behind the front and rear wheel arches on each side.

In 1960 independent rear suspension was adopted in the TRI/60 Testa Rossa models and still they won virtually everything in sight. In 1961 they were effectively replaced by the mid-engined 246SP V6 machines, at least for the works teams.

Although unsophisticated, the Berkeley had its own charm . . .

Berkeley
1959, Great Britain

Berkeley Cars Ltd of Biggleswade, Bedfordshire built a line of small-capacity sports cars during the late-fifties which were just about as diametrically opposed to, for example, the fearsome Allards as anyone could imagine. Berkeley were essentially a caravan manufacturer and they adopted in 1956 a Laurie Bond design for a motor-cycle-engined sports car. This incorporated front-wheel chain drive of the type Bond had adopted as early as 1948 in his own cars. The chassis/body structure was moulded in glass-fibre resin; the car employed independent suspension at front and rear with swing axles at the back.

Berkeley bought in air-cooled motor-cycle power from Anzani (322 cc), Excelsior (328 cc twin and 492 cc three-cylinder) and Royal-Enfield (692 cc four-stroke), this last model in tuned form being good for a fearsome 90 mph. Berkeley also built a 328 cc three-wheeler version.

In 1960 development was carried out on a more conventional vehicle, using a 997 cc Ford of Dagenham 105E Anglia water-cooled engine, but it appeared too late to save the concern which ceased production in 1961.

It would be an overstatement to say that there was not a dry eye in the house upon Berkeley's collapse as a motor-manufacturing concern, for although their cars were always sweet little things, they were in many respects very spartan and crude and their ultimate handling certainly left much to be desired. Still, some were exported to the highly critical American market where the influential magazine *Road & Track* said it all by heading their road test of the car, 'You Can't Send the Kid Up in a Crate Like That!'.

Jaguar E-Type
1961, Great Britain

When the E-Type Jaguar was unveiled as a replacement for the XK150 series in the spring of 1961 it was greeted with acclaim from the whole motoring world. William Lyons's rare eye for graceful styling had produced a svelte design which brought into reality almost every enthusiast's dream of the ultimate sports car.

Jaguar had developed their D-Type monocoque centre-section theme in an interim prototype sports-racing car which had raced in Briggs Cunningham's white and blue American colours at Le Mans in 1960. The E-Type now used the 3781 cc XK twin-overhead-camshaft six-cylinder engine in 265 bhp trim, and carried all-independent suspension, at last replacing the live rear axle of the Cs, Ds, and 120s, 140s and 150s. Disc brakes also appeared all round; at the rear they were located inboard on the cheeks of the final-drive unit. Open roadster and coupé body-styles were available; the fixed-head coupé was the fastest model on independent road test—though carefully prepared by the Coventry works—achieving a genuine 151 mph. Such performance was available for the remarkably low price of £2196 but insurance companies reacted by heavily loading drivers they thought too young, too inexperienced, or simply suspect.

The E-Type became *the* sports car of the sixties, exemplifying all that was best in British high-performance car engineering, although the early 3.8-litre models were always handicapped by their slow, heavy old Moss four-speed gearbox. This was replaced in 1965 by a superb all-synchromesh gearbox in conjunction with an enlarged 4235 cc engine, and in 1966 the 2 + 2 Coupé was introduced with raised and rather ungainly roofline to accommodate occasional rear-seat passengers. In 1970 another new model was introduced, based on a long 2 + 2 wheelbase; with 5.3-litre V12 power, this was the ultimate E-Type Jaguar, although the clean-cut styling of the original models had long since been despoiled by American Federal Safety Regulation requirements.

Not a lot of space, but bags of grace and pace typified the Jaguar E-Type, particularly the early 3.8-litre roadsters as seen here racing at Brands Hatch.

Lotus Elite
1961, Great Britain

Colin Chapman's Lotus Engineering company grew from a part-time hobby building trials specials in the late forties and early fifties into a company which dominated the competition world, thanks to Chapman's advanced thinking on chassis and suspension design. His aerodynamic-bodied, ultra-light-weight sports-racing cars set new standards during the fifties, and in the middle of the decade Chapman began to plan production of a road-going flagship model to capitalize upon his prestige and competition success.

This model, the Lotus Type 14 Elite, made its debut in 1957 and was not only startlingly attractive but also of absorbing technical interest. It was the first Lotus intended primarily for road use, and yet naturally it retained immense competition potential. It was based upon a fully stressed monocoque body/chassis unit which was unique in being constructed entirely of glass-fibre mouldings; the sophisticated all-independent suspension was bolted onto strong-points moulded into the structure. For structural reasons the car was only offered as a fixed-head coupé. Power was provided by a 1216cc Coventry Climax single-overhead-camshaft engine delivering about 75bhp and this endowed the good-looking and very lightweight projectile with a standard top speed of some 112mph. Disc brakes were fitted all round.

Unfortunately the Elite proved a pretty deceiver, certainly of its manufacturer, for production costs were far higher than anticipated and minimal profit was shown on each one built; very soon Lotus was selling the cars at a loss. The unique plastic body structure proved vulnerable to fatigue cracks and many customers became disgruntled, but on the racing circuits of the world the Lotus Elite proved itself a formidable contender in the 1300cc class, winning its class at Nürburgring in 1959, and at Le Mans every year from 1959 to 1964.

Today the better-maintained surviving Lotus Elites are much-prized collectors' cars and they are still raced with tremendous success at amateur level in Britain, Europe, Australia, the Far East and America.

All Lotus cars bear the unmistakeable stamp of the firm's founder, Anthony Colin Bruce Chapman, and the Lotus badge carries his initials.

Triumph TR4
1962, Great Britain

Perhaps the Triumph TR range of inexpensive sports cars, economical to run, yet with undoubted high performance, reached its peak with the introduction of the muscular TR4 model in September 1962. By that time over 80,000 TR3 and TR3As had been produced and the new model, with its square-cut, chunky Italian styling by Michelotti, proved a worthy replacement.

It used the trusty Triumph four-cylinder engine in 2138cc form, developing 105bhp gross at 4600rpm, which was transmitted via a very pleasant-to-operate, four-speed-and-reverse, all-synchromesh gearbox. The independent front suspension with coil springs was retained from the model's immediate predecessor, the TR3A, along with the live rear axle on half-elliptic leaf-springs. The TR4 was based upon a slightly wider chassis frame than that used in the TR3 family, and proved very attractive upon its introduction, reasonably priced at £1095 in open form and £1146 as a closed two-seat coupé. A detachable 'Surrey top' proved an unusual innovation, the roof panel alone detaching to leave a fixed rear

screen still in place. Wind-up side windows completed the cockpit protection.

The new model had a 0–50mph acceleration time of just over seven seconds, which was quite brisk in those days; it could cover the standing-start quarter mile in 17.5 seconds, and had a top speed of about 110mph.

In January 1965 the TR4A was announced, this being the first all-independently-suspended sports car in the TR range. It used the Triumph 2000 saloon-car independent rear suspension with trailing-arm and coil springs; with 104bhp it was slightly heavier than the TR4 which it replaced, 40,300 TR4s having been produced. The TR4A was never quite a match for the TR4 either in a straight line or around corners, but it rode more comfortably and was more refined. Some 28,500 TR4As were built before the model's disappearance in August 1968, the fuel-injection TR5 and restyled TR6 continuing the tradition until the advent of the modern TR7 coupé in the seventies.

Austin-Healey 3000
1963, Great Britain

When the 2.6-litre Austin-Healey 100–6 was announced in 1956, it was obvious that its sales potential could be greatly enhanced by the competition possibilities of the six-cylinder engine. However, the bodyshell used by the 100–6 was more a 2 + 2 than a traditional two-seat roadster, offering shelf space behind the front seats for two small children or a 'transverse normal adult'. This made the car some 450lb heavier than the basic four-cylinder Austin-Healey 100, but weight was trimmed with great success by the British Motor Corporation competitions department at Abingdon, who took the 100–6 and modified it not for racing, but for the arduous sport of rallying.

Thus the 'Big Healey' came into existence in rally trim, finished in the factory colours of red and white, and festooned with long-range driving lamps and spotlights. The raucous six-cylinder cars came into their own after 1959 when the engine was taken out to 2912cc to produce the Austin-Healey 3000. By 1965 this power unit was delivering a reliable 160bhp, while the body and chassis proved robust enough to withstand the worst buffets and batterings of the roughest international rally conditions. Essentially the rally Healeys were excellent high-speed open-road competition cars, but when driven in the early sixties (notably by dirt-road-bred Finnish aces like Timo Makinen) they also made their mark on loose-surface forest stages in such gruelling events as the British RAC Rally.

In 1961 and 1962, crewed notably by Stirling's sister Pat Moss with Ann Wisdom, and by the Morley twins Donald and Earle, the big Healeys won the testing Liège-Rome-Liège, and in 1964 the Austrian Alpine Rally. The production road-going versions basked in the reflected glory of these achievements until February 1968, by which time over 50,000 of the large-engined Austin-Healeys had been built.

Sadly, management panicked at the introduction of restrictive legislation in the large American export market, killing off the Healeys in favour of the misbegotten three-litre-engined MGC. Datsun in Japan studied the Healey theme, and updated it in their very successful 240Z, showing what could have been done with just a little enterprise.

▲ *At its best when sitting down under power, the Austin-Healey 3000 rally car in the rain on one Epreuve.*

▶ *The legend of the 'Big Healey' grew in the forest rallies of the late fifties and sixties in Britain and on the open road rally races of the Continent. Here in the forests that barking three-litre six-cylinder scatters loose stones as a works driver powers out of a curve.*

MGB
1963, Great Britain

Sydney Enever's technical team at Abingdon developed their first unitary-construction monocoque sports car for release in 1962, replacing the separate-chassis MGA. This model, known logically enough as the 'MGB', did not win itself instant affection from the MG test-drivers. Whereas the MGA had been a forgiving and good-handling car right from prototype the Abingdon company had teething troubles with the MGB in making the chassis structure sufficiently rigid to offer predictable handling qualities and adequate controllability. After a fairly fraught development period the car was licked into shape, and the 1795 cc 95 bhp MGB was released to the public in 1962 – offered as a two-seat roadster – and in October 1965 a fixed-roof MGB GT coupé joined the range.

The MGB was a handsome-looking car with an appeal quite different from that of the flowingly styled, almost glamorous little MGA. It remained in production with few apparent changes other than those dictated by new safety regulations in its major markets until 1980, when MG in its existing form was killed off by its parent, the British Leyland group. By this time the MGB was old-fashioned and obsolescent, even though market demand was still very high.

Certainly the MGB once properly developed formed a solid, road-going sports car with good handling, and many competition variants appeared which did quite well up to the late-sixties in minor long-distance sports-car races and the occasional rally.

The car sold very well in the USA until in cut-price deference to new safety regulations vast impact-absorbing bumpers had to be added to the existing bodyshells and, more serious, they had to be located at a regulation minimum height. To achieve this level, the export MGB version was jacked up on its suspension into the air; in this form, further

hindered by smog-limiting emission-control devices which strangled the engine's already rather modest power output, the poor MGB not only did not like going round corners, but also had barely sufficient power to step smartly along the straights.

Shelby-American Cobra
1964, United States/Great Britain

Large-engined sports cars have always had a special appeal for American enthusiast drivers, and in the early sixties Carroll Shelby (formerly with the Aston Martin works team and winner at Le Mans in 1959) decided that he was going to build just such a car. He looked around Europe for a suitable vehicle for a cheap-to-buy, easy-to-maintain yet very powerful, proprietary American V8 engine, and he chose the AC Ace chassis and body being built at Thames Ditton.

In 1962 the first Shelby American prototype cars were constructed, mating a 4.2-litre Ford V8 from Detroit with the British twin-tube chassis and pert Ferrari Barchetta-derived bodyshell. Initial experience of these Anglo-American hybrids showed-up – predictably – handling and strength problems which were rapidly remedied, although the cars always remained demanding machines to drive really quickly.

After 75 of these Cobra sports cars had been built, the 4.2-litre Ford engine was replaced in 1963 by the latest 4.7-litre variant which offered 195 bhp. In England the cars were known as AC Cobras, while in the USA Shelby American took full credit with no mention at all of the AC parentage.

By 1965 Shelby was shoe-horning the latest 6989 cc Ford V8 engine into further-improved Cobra shells. These were more bulbous, with extended wheel-arch eyebrows

▼ *Shelby American intended their Cobra to be 'all bear' and succeeded.*

to enclose ever-wider wheels and tyres, and with suspensions uprated to accommodate the seven-litre engine's greater mass and power output, which hovered around the 345 bhp mark. Acceleration and braking in a straight line was shattering, 0-100-0-100-0 mph being achieved in less than 30 seconds! Identified by their 289- and 427 cubic-inch capacities respectively, the 4.7- and seven-litre Cobras were literally earth-shaking devices, although in competition around corners drivers claimed they had to shut their eyes and hope. Even the smaller car could punch itself from rest to 60 mph in 5.5 seconds, and reach 138 mph flat-out. A special Daytona coupé competition model with enveloping bodywork was constructed with a 380 bhp 4.7-litre engine – this was capable of 195 mph. Construction of all models ceased in 1968.

Exhausting drive – Dan Gurney's Cobra in the 1964 Targa Florio.

KYB847C

Morgan
1965, Great Britain

The remarkable Morgan Motor Company has survived into the eighties with an ever-faithful band of enthusiasts queuing up to buy its sports cars, which are still constructed in the traditional manner. Their ash-framed bodies feature separate flowing wings and running boards, and offer fairly spartan accommodation. Morgans even today have a 'thirties' character they are still 'the real thing', and not by any means a replica.

Under the direction of Peter Morgan, son of 'H.F.S.' the founder, the Malvern Link company developed during the fifties, building first a Plus Four model fitted with the tuned 70hp Standard Vanguard engine, and later, from 1954, a 90bhp Triumph TR2 engine which provided genuine 100mph performance for the first time.

In 1955 a small Morgan was reintroduced, fitting into the range below the Plus Four and using the faithful 1172cc side-valve Ford four-cylinder engine which had powered the

Opposite lock – this Morgan Plus Eight was an optimistic entry in the 1980 Monte Carlo Rally, practising here at Shelsley Walsh.

old F4 Morgan three-wheeler, discontinued in 1950. This new four-wheel model was known as the 4/4 Series 2; later the overhead-valve Ford 105E engine was substituted as Dagenham dropped the side-valve.

Meanwhile the Plus Four kept pace with Triumph TR engine development. A stream-lined coupé model very similar in general appearance to the Lotus Elite was offered in 1964 to a roar of disapproval from the Morgan traditionalists, and from 1968 into the eighties to date Morgan have used the quiet, reliable and excellent Rover $3\frac{1}{2}$-litre V8 engine in their Plus-Eight model, capable of a comfortable 125 mph on its large wheels and tyres without losing any of the age-old Morgan character.

In many ways Morgan is an anachronism in a modern motoring world – but Thank God for Independence and the retention of old standards of workmanship and pride.

Ford Mustang
1966, United States

The Ford Motor Company's answer to Chevrolet's early success with the Corvette was the Thunderbird, introduced in 1955. This handsome if not exactly sporting machine was larger and more powerful than the Corvette, with 4.8 litres, 200 bhp and 115 mph. However, instead of continuing the two-seat roadster theme, Ford backed out of the market in 1958, modified the Thunderbird range to carry four seats and so killed it as a 'sports car'.

At the United States Grand Prix meeting at Watkins Glen in 1962, Ford's engineers displayed a two-seat mid-engined roadster exercise which they called the 'Mustang'. In very different form, the Mustang emerged in production in 1963 as a compact front-engined four-seater offered with a massive range of optional equipment. This allowed the successful young man or woman to personalize the car to choice, making it as sporty or as civilized as they wished. The Mustang was available with six- and eight-cylinder engines in four sizes from 2781 cc to 4728 cc and with power output ranging from 101 bhp to 210 bhp. The Mustang in these various forms was good for anything from 95 mph to a full-blooded 120 mph; and when Carroll Shelby adopted the model and 'breathed upon it', he produced the Shelby Mustang GT350 with modified bodywork, engine, suspension, brakes, fittings and trim. The road variant gave 306 bhp and the competition model 350 bhp from the 4.7-litre V8 engine, Ford's famous '289' cubic-inch unit. In 1967 Shelby introduced the GT500 with the full seven-litre V8 giving 360 bhp in road tune or 400 bhp for the race track. Even the road car could top 135 mph and still a vast range of options was available to normal owners who would never dream of hazarding their production Mustangs in competition.

The Ford Mustang featured strongly in competition saloon car racing in Britain, Europe and the USA in the mid-sixties, but in truth it was essentially a modern 'sporting', rather than 'sports', car.

Works Ford rally Mustangs slamming past the Reims pits during a sixties Tour de France Automobile.

Ford GT40
1968, Great Britain

Ford of America began to realize in the early sixties just how much the masculine and youthful image of motor racing could boost their car sales. The Mustang development was aimed at a 'youth' market, for the post-war baby boom had produced a new car market with a low average age. Ford supplied this market very successfully, and in order to gain prestige and a glowing competition image rapidly they even attempted, in 1962–63, to take over the Ferrari company in Italy. Mr Ferrari had no heir and was worried about the future for his creation. Ford could assure that future, but, Mr Ferrari decided, only at too great a cost to his own and to Italy's prestige.

Thus rebuffed the Ford Motor Company decided to release funds to take on Ferrari at his own game. Their prime objective was the Le Mans 24-Hours race, with Indianapolis as a secondary target. Coincidentally in 1963 the British specialist company of Lola Cars under Eric Broadley had developed a mid-engined competition coupé car powered by a 4.2-litre Ford V8 engine. Ford arranged to absorb the Lola project to save time on development of their own GT, which was

being produced under the aegis of engineer Roy Lunn. The first Ford GT40 (so named because it stood only 40 inches high) was completed in 1964 but suffered immense and mortifying teething troubles which came close to making Ford a laughing stock. Certainly Mr Ferrari could not resist a smile at their expense.

In 1965 this Anglo-American project neared fruition, with Ford Advanced Vehicles at Slough, England, building the cars which were then raced largely under US management and guidance. With 4.7-litre V8 engines, victory came at Daytona in 1965, but the cars failed with seven-litre power at Le Mans. In 1966 seven-litre Mark II cars won Le Mans, and in 1967 the different, but still seven-litre-powered, Mark IV cars were victorious for Ford. Meanwhile the GT40 basic design had been developed around 4.7-5.0 litre V8 engines as Group 4 production sports cars, and the self-same car, chassis '1074', won Le Mans in 1967 and 1968. About 112 cars were built in all, and today they are all collectors' pieces, much prized 200 mph grand tourers.

De Tomaso Pantera
1971, Italy

Alejandro de Tomaso, an Argentinian, first came to prominence in the mid-fifties as a racing driver, campaigning OSCAs built by the Maserati brothers. He married wealthy

American lady driver Isabel Haskell and together they were to become a considerable force on the Italian motoring scene, as they came to control Maserati and Innocenti, among other concerns, in the late seventies.

De Tomaso began building cars of his own in small quantities in the early sixties. He started with the Vallelunga GT coupé, named after the Roman race-track, using a 1½-litre Ford Cortina engine mounted amidships and about 50 Vallelungas were produced before he became more ambitious and developed a more powerful, but largely similar, device using a Carroll Shelby-tuned 4.7-litre Ford Cobra V8 engine giving some 305 bhp.

In 1967 De Tomaso took an interest in the famous Ghia styling house, and Ghia developed an ultra-low and excitingly exotic body-shape for the new car, which De Tomaso named the Mangusta. This was a rather crude device, difficult to handle, despite its good looks and considerable potential. It could reach 145 mph in a rather wobbly straight line and accelerated from rest to 60 mph in a blistering 6.1 seconds.

The Mangusta went into series production for the American market, being modified to accord with ever-changing US Safety and Emission Regulations as the months passed. In 1969 De Tomaso's plant in Modena was turning out about 20 Mangustas a month, and the Argentinian had forged a US marketing link with the Ford Motor Company.

Vignale, another of the great Italian styling houses, came under his umbrella and after the failure of a coupé named the Mustela and powered by a 2.9-litre V6 British Ford engine, De Tomaso bounced back with the American Ford V8-engined Pantera two-door mid-engined coupé. With 5.8 litres and 330 bhp this fearsome device was again handsome and very fast but suffered various quality and handling problems which did not rest comfortably with 162 mph speed. Many Panteras were raced, however, and found an enthusiastic following among the braver enthusiasts, especially in the USA.

Matra 530
1970, France

Engins Matra is a giant French aerospace company, primarily concerned with advanced rocketry and systems but in 1964 it acquired the failing René Bonnet racing-car company to gain international publicity. Matra Sports was established in 1965 to continue development of the Bonnet Formula 3 monocoque-chassis racing cars and to run the existing Renault-engined sports models. Production cars initially followed the René Bonnet stream-lined coupé theme using glass-fibre reinforced resin bodyshells and Gordini-tuned Renault engines. In 1966 the Djet, as the car was called, could achieve 109 mph thanks to good aerodynamics. In 1967 the car was uprated to use a 1250cc 105 bhp Renault engine and a new 2 + 2 car appeared with a 1.7-litre Ford Taunus V4 engine amidships. This year, incidentally, was the beginning of a period of Matra success on the race-track.

In 1968 the Djet was dropped and the angular-bodied 530 production coupe took prominence, a closed sports car of good aerodynamic shape, with good handling and performance. During 1969 Ford of Cologne produced a new V4 engine which was adopted for the 530 coupe, but Matra were already discussing a takeover by Chrysler-Simca which later went through. So Matra-Simca came into existence and the Ford engine tie-up had to cease. In 1973 a new Chrysler 1294cc transverse mid-engined car replaced the 530 – this three abreast model was named the 'Bagheera'.

The Ferrari Dino is a classic in the mid-engined tradition, V6 engine and Pininfarina bodywork being combined with superb road-holding.

Ferrari Dino 246GT
1970, Italy

Enzo and Laura Ferrari's only son was christened Alfredo after his uncle, Enzo's brother, who had died of natural causes during World War I. In Italian 'Alfredino' is the affectionate form of this christian name, and the diminutive of Alfredino is simply 'Dino'. Poor Dino Ferrari died from complications of progressive muscular dystrophy in 1956. Within months of his death a new 1500cc V6 Formula 2 engine was running on the Maranello test-beds, and Mr Ferrari decreed that this engine should carry the name Dino after his beloved son; in 1958 Ferrari Dino V6 Grand Prix cars carried Mike Hawthorn to his World Drivers' Championship title.

In 1959 Dino V6 engines powered sports and Formula 1 cars and by 1961 Ferrari V6s were in a position to win the World Championship again. During the sixties a string of developing V6 and V8 engines carried the Dino name, and come 1967 and the introduction of a new 1600cc Formula 2, Ferrari wanted access to a production engine from which a racing Formula 2 unit could be developed. He sold Fiat the idea of their building

Cromodora cast-alloy road wheel for the Ferrari Dino.

a production version of his two-litre V6 so that he could 'modify it for racing' and so slide what was effectively a purebred 1600 cc racing engine around the new Formula 2 rules. He was successful, although the Formula 2 cars were not, until the end of 1968.

At that time the road-going small Ferrari, using the two-litre Dino V6 engine, was introduced as an exotic but inexpensive car wearing pretty Pininfarina bodywork. This model was later updated to accommodate a full 2.4-litre 246GT V6 engine, and in spider and coupé forms these Dinos proved mouth-watering road cars offering tremendous performance and superb road-holding. The V6 engine was set transversely amidships behind the two-seat cockpit, and the little cars were good for 140 mph with acceleration to match. Their steel bodies have proved subject to rust and decay, which is a tragedy, for they are truly glorious little machines and the seventies' supreme embodiment of the sports-car tradition. They were discontinued in 1973, and replaced by three-litre transverse V8-engined Dino models.

Dino was run as a marque separate from Ferrari, until production outran that of their larger brethren. This was an interesting

Pininfarina's reverse-curved rear screen was a fascinating styling feature of the Ferrari Dino family's beautiful bodywork.

point for Ferrari dealers and importers around the world considered that to create a 'Dino' marque was itself a marketing error, for their customers required true Ferraris and were put off by the idea of buying something which was regarded by owners of the more expensive and larger models as 'not a proper Ferrari'. In truth, however, the Dino name had achieved enough in competition to be truly honourable.

In fact it was the Dino cars which introduced truly modern chassis engineering into the Ferrari tradition, for while the larger, predominantly V12-engined Ferraris had superb engines and gearboxes their handling and cornering behaviour was often 'antique' at best and 'truck-like' at worst. With the svelte little Dino range Ferrari really offered adequate, indeed outstanding road-holding in the modern idiom, and that development made an immense difference to this most classical of post-war classic manufacturers.

Lamborghini Miura
1972, Italy

During the sixties the Italian tractor manufacturer Ferruccio Lamborghini took to car manufacture more or less as a hobby. He pursued his enthusiasm for matchless cars and created a line of luxurious, very high-performance Grand Touring cars which achieved the highest standards of technical sophistication.

The first Lamborghini car appeared at the Turin Show of 1963. It was a front-engined GT coupé using a $3\frac{1}{2}$-litre four-cam V12 engine with six Weber carburetters. This very Ferrari-like device looked more like a true racing than a production road-going unit, the whole project being supervised by ex-Ferrari engineers Giotto Bizzarini and Gian Paolo Dall'ara.

Italian exoticar – Lamborghini Espada.

After unforeseen problems in preparing the Lamborghini 350GT for production it began to appear in numbers in the mid-sixties. Meanwhile Dall'ara had produced an even more exciting design in the Miura – named after the pugnacious Spanish breed of fighting bull, Lamborghini's response to Enzo Ferrari's Prancing Horse.

This strikingly unconventional Miura packed a four-litre V12 engine set transversely behind the two-seat cockpit amidships, driving through spur gears to the clutch and five-speed transaxle assembly. This remarkable assem-blage produced and handled no less than 420 bhp at 8000 rpm, and yet with simply incredible reliability and lack of temperament the car could poodle around city streets or streak along the Autostrada del Sole at anything up to a genuine 180 mph. It was the World's fastest production car for some time.

In the seventies the Miura's crown was inherited by the remarkably uncompromising Lamborghini Countach of generally similar specification, which takes its name from a Modenese slang word meaning more or less 'Corr . . .'; and with reason.

Lola T212
1972, Great Britain

Former architect Eric Broadley began his competition-car construction company in the late fifties more or less as a hobby. He had built himself a club-special which he named 'Lolita', and the 'Lola' cars which followed were built on the precept that whatever Lola wants, Lola gets.

During the sixties Lola Cars Ltd worked briefly with the mighty Ford Motor Company of Dearborn, Michigan, to develop the original GT40 model, and that programme really established Broadley's company in fit form to 'go it alone'. Currently – in 1979-80 – Lola Cars of Huntingdon are the world's largest manufacturer of pure competition cars, building sports and single-seater models for virtually every International racing class.

The European two-litre Championship came to prominence in the sports car world in 1970 and remained there for five years during which time Lola products featured strongly. Broadley's Lola T212 design, for example, featured a central monocoque chassis which carried its Cosworth-Ford four-cylinder FVC engine of 1790 cc (and yet 245 bhp!) in a tubular cradle behind the cockpit. All-independent suspension featured, as was conventional competition practice, with coil-spring/damper units and wishbone location. Gearbox was a proprietary Hewland five-speed transaxle. These cars gained considerable success in Britain and western Europe while many were sold to the USA for club racing there. In 1972 the Lola T290 version appeared with cleaned-up, sharper-nosed body lines; the Cosworth BDA or FVC engines were taken out to as much as 1930 cc and produced over 250 bhp at 9500 rpm. In 1973 this model was followed by the T292 with a large wing over the tail and lengthened nose, with 275 bhp Cosworth power. The 1974 model was a further improved car known as the T294, while in 1975 completely revised aerodynamic thinking produced the T390 with curved and bulbous lines reminiscent of an Alpine-Renault.

Throughout all these years the two-litre Lolas were amongst the best-selling of a modern sports-racing line, directly in the tradition of the Lotus, Jaguar, Aston Martin and MG racers of the fifties and before.

Alpine-Renault A110
1973, France

Automobiles Alpine was founded at Dieppe by Jean Redélé in 1955. He was an enthusiastic Renault dealer who that year built a competition-orientated special using Renault components. The car promptly featured successfully in the small-car class of the classic Italian Mille Miglia race. He used moulded glass-fibre bodywork for his cars, offering them as two and four-seat coupés.

In 1961 Redélé offered two new body styles, one a 2 + 2 GT coupé and the other a very aerodynamic two-seat Berlinette. The glassfibre bodywork of the latter was mounted upon a central-backbone chassis which carried the one-litre Renault engine in various tune-states and forms at its extreme tail, behind the rear axle line. Redélé called the Berlinette the A110 'Tour de France' after the great speed competition for GT cars still being held in France and immediately neighbouring countries each autumn.

The A110 actually set out with only 850cc and less than 50bhp to propel it, but Redélé became increasingly confident as success

followed success, Renault showed increasing interest, and their engine consultant Amédée Gordini produced ever more effective competition power units for the Dieppe factory's use. Renault 8, then Renault 16, and finally very highly-tuned 1800cc power units developing close on 200bhp were slotted into the sleek little competition coupé's tail. The chassis were well-balanced, extremely agile, and responded magnificently when asked to change direction or dodge suddenly. They were also far, far stronger than they looked, and these attributes rendered them magnificently suitable for International rallying, in which the Alpines' extraordinary agility gave them the edge over often far more powerful rivals. In 1973 the works Alpine-Renault team from Dieppe won the prestigious World Rally Championships.

The A110 was finally removed from the catalogues in 1977, to be replaced by the less attractive-looking A310 model. The A110 was a modern classic sports car by any standards, and sadly missed.

TVR Vixen
1973, Great Britain

The Lancastrian specialist sports-car company, TVR, derives its name from that of its originator, Trevor Wilkinson, who began building tube chassis and later complete car kits in the late 1950s. His tiny Blackpool works produced

a two-seat coupé known as the Grantura, with a glass-fibre body, powered by Coventry Climax or Ford 100E engines and suspended on Volkswagen components. In 1960 the

Mark II Grantura retained the same basic body shape–which has proved timeless–but adopted Ford 105E and MGA additional power units. John Turner devised a new Mark III tubular chassis frame with double-wishbone suspension in 1962 and these TVRs from Blackpool really began to make a name for themselves in minor-level club races and rallies.

Meanwhile the TVR company itself had undergone many management and ownership changes, but the little Blackpool-built cars soldiered through good times and bad with adequate success. A Ford V8-engined Anglo-American model known as the TVR Griffith was produced in conjunction with an American promoter, and after his company collapsed TVR continued V8 production.

Trevor Fiore designed a graceful and very Italianate new body style in 1965, which was later developed as a separate (and unsuccessful) marque using the large Austin-Healey chassis and running gear. In 1966 TVR produced their Mark IV with 1800 MGB power unit and in 1968 a move was made downmarket with the little Tina, using Fiore bodystyling and a Hillman Imp engine. The 1800S model was also offered with Ford Cortina power–which was a very practical proposition–and they called this model the TVR Vixen.

Come the seventies and a Triumph-engined 2500M appeared, fitting a new multi-tubular backbone chassis frame under that so-familiar but still not dated body style. In 1972 this chassis was applied to all TVR engine options and later in the decade a convertible appeared, together with a Turbo version, using a highly tuned, turbocharged Ford V8 power unit.

Triumph Spitfire Mk IV
1973, Great Britain

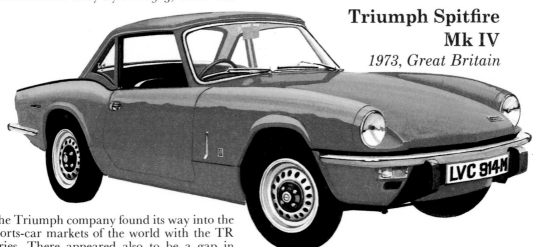

The Triumph company found its way into the sports-car markets of the world with the TR series. There appeared also to be a gap in the market for an inexpensive, small-capacity sporting car, easy to drive and not too fast–just the thing in fact for the youthful or lady enthusiast who liked the sporting idea if not the full-blown practice.

In October 1962 Triumph released the Spitfire 4, an 1147 cc two-seat model developed from the successful Herald saloon with its backbone chassis. Styling was by the Italian house of Michelotti; mechanically there was little difference from the Herald except for the use of softer springs to accommodate the lightweight body. A twin-SU-carburettor version of the Herald 1200 engine was used, producing 63 bhp at 5740 rpm. Rack-and-pinion steering gave the minute turning circle of only 24 feet and the four-speed gearbox with synchomesh on all but first gear was another attraction. This little car was good for 93 mph, would reach 50 mph from

rest in around 12 seconds and its fuel consumption was a major selling point at 35 mpg. It was priced at £729 and sold very well.

From September 1963 overdrive and a hardtop were available for the now best-selling little Spitfire, and in March 1965 an improved Mark II Spitfire offered a 67 bhp engine, improved trim and furnishing, and was altogether a less spartan device. Fastback coupé versions were raced at Le Mans with some success in the 24-Hours endurance race and in October 1966 the Spitfire-based two-litre Triumph GT6 coupé was announced. In early 1967 the Spitfire was itself uprated to house a 1296 cc engine; with 70 bhp at 6000 rpm this Mark III version offered 95 mph, and a 0–50 mph time of around 10 seconds–still with 36 mpg fuel consumption. A Mark IV, with changes in styling and mechanical detail, followed in 1970.

Datsun 240Z
1975, Japan

During the sixties the Japanese motor industry slammed into world wide export markets with shattering effect. Companies like Datsun and Toyota proved extremely adept at producing practical and reliable motor-cars to a price, and with back-up service which the average customer could not afford to ignore. The Japanese also looked at the performance-car field, and Datsun in particular scored a notable success with their 240Z coupé model.

The Kwaishinsha works had produced its first car in 1912 in Tokyo, and in 1914 a more successful second car was produced which the company named the Dat, using the initials of the proprietors, K. Den, R. Aoyama and A.

Works Datsun 240Z rally car at home in the rugged and dusty conditions of the East African Safari Rally.

Takeuchi. In 1926 Kwaishinsha merged with Jitsuyo Jidosha Seizo to form the Dat Automobile Manufacturing Company of Osaka, actually making trucks. When car production resumed in 1931 they were called Datson ('son of Dat'), but in order to suggest the national Japanese emblem of the rising sun the name assumed its final form, Datsun, in 1932.

Immediately after World War II Datsun cars were based on the American Crosley design and during the fifties the company built nothing less (nor more) than the Austin A50 under licence. It was during the sixties that Nissan Datsun modernized their range and attacked international markets so successfully while the market at home was heavily protected against imports.

Effectively the 240Z coupé was the result of examination of the Austin-Healey 3000 six-cylinder model, which had been allowed to wither on the vine in the face of stringent new US Federal Safety Regulations in 1968. Datsun developed their own 2.4-litre single-overhead-camshaft six-cylinder unit enclosed in strikingly attractive streamlined coupé bodywork; with five-speed all-synchromesh transmission, all-independent suspension, front disc brakes and 160 bhp the big Datsun carried on where the big Healey had been allowed to die. The 240Z was fast, handled adequately well, was quite economical and very reliable – very much a sports car for the seventies.

Triumph TR7
1975, Great Britain

The long line of Triumph TR sporting cars had developed as far as the long-nose TR6, when, in January 1975, the two-door two-seat coupé TR7 replaced the old traditional line with its directly traceable 'fifties' pedigree.

The new TR7 coupé was designed very much with the American market in mind, which in part excuses the exaggerated wedge-shape profile with ugly, sculptured indentation in the body sides. The wheelbase, at only 7 ft 3 in, was rather too short for comfort when combined with a 4 ft 7 in track front and rear, and the result was a car which, though nimble and quick to change direction, rode rather choppily and felt a little unstable along any bumpy straight.

It was marketed as the 'front-engined car with the mid-engined looks' but in truth combined perhaps the worst points of both designs. Its four-cylinder engine with a single overhead camshaft displaced 1998 cc and developed about 80 bhp at 5400 rpm. A four-speed manual gearbox transmitted power to the rear wheels. The bodywork was an all-steel unitary structure with independent front suspension and a live rear axle, on coil-springs all round. Disc brakes featured at the front and drums at the rear, with dual hydraulic circuits and vacuum servo assistance. This little car was claimed to have a 108 mph top speed, not half as fast as its appearance implied, but it has proved reasonably successful both in the USA and in Europe.

The basic TR7 was progressively updated by the introduction of a five-speed gearbox and later by the installation of the Rover 3500 V8 light-alloy engine which at last gave it real power. Known as the TR8 in this guise, the car was rallied extensively by a works team with some success, and in British Airways sponsorship livery the TR8's certainly looked the part as their drivers fought their way with visible excesses of power around the rally stages of the world.

Fiat X1/9
1976, Italy

During the seventies the sporting car in general developed as a two-seater coupé. American Safety Regulations at one time looked likely to ban the open-top car for good, hence Triumph's replacement of the TR6 by what was in original form a coupé-only TR7, and Jaguar's replacement of the É-Type roadster by the XJ-S coupé-only model. Some manufacturers were less cautious, and Porsche developed the so-called Targa top in which the fixed windscreen surround was augmented by a roll-over bar-cum-rear-screen surround behind the cockpit, and a rigid but detachable roof panel was provided to insert between them. This system had appeared in the Triumph TR-series 'Surrey top' but Porsche gave it its modern name following their successes in the arduous Targa Florio race around Sicily. This race favoured open-cockpit cars, which nevertheless had to retain good aerodynamic shape for the long Buon-fornello Straight along the coastline.

In fact it was upon the Targa Florio circuit in Sicily that Fiat first introduced their extraordinary X1/9 Targa-top sports car to the world's motoring press. What this vast manufacturer of utility cars had done was to take the transverse engine and front-wheel-drive package from the existing and very successful Fiat 128 and install it amidships behind the two-seat cockpit of a striking, wedge-profiled bodyshell both designed and made for them by the house of Bertone, at Grugliasco outside Turin. The rigid roof panel could be removed and stowed away in the front locker and thus converted the figure-hugging little X1/9 proved

And everything opens! Fiat's X1/9 was a daring gamble which paid tremendous dividends for Fiat and stylist-cum-body-builder Bertone.

to be a staggeringly enjoyable little car.

The high-revving 1300cc four-cylinder engine could punch the car along at speeds as high as 103mph, and it would accelerate from 0–60mph in about 12.6 seconds. It covered the standing-start kilometre in 34.5 seconds, which was a very worthy achievement, returning an albeit modest 21.5–28mpg. Disc brakes on all four wheels were without the servo which in other Fiat models had proved disturbingly harsh in operation, and the X1/9 set new standards for nimble and agile handling, controllability, braking and general driving fun in the very best sports-car traditions.

In 1978 a 1.5-litre version was added to the range and as the eighties dawn the baby Fiat is still very attractive to all who enjoy their motoring.

Lotus Esprit
1979, Great Britain

The Lotus Elite ceased production in 1963, to be replaced by the more practical Elan, and later the Europa mid-engined coupé. In due course, too, a new Elite was offered, with a Vauxhall-based engine developed by Lotus.

At the Turin Motor Show in 1972 Giorgetto Giugiaro's Ital-Design styling house produced a mid-engined study which placed the new Lotus engine behind the two-seat cockpit of à sleek and very low-slung coupé of gorgeous appearance. Colin Chapman was very interested in this project, and detailed engineers Tony Rudd and Mike Kimberley to form a team to develop a production variant of this Italian study. Working closely with Giugiaro in Turin, Lotus evolved their striking Esprit two-seater which was introduced in October 1975.

The four-cylinder engine of 95.2mm bore × 69.2mm stroke displaces 1973cc and carries twin overhead camshafts actuating four valves per cylinder. Peak power is 160bhp at 6200 rpm and this is delivered to the rear wheels via a five-speed gearbox. The Esprit uses a backbone chassis frame with all-independent suspension front and rear based directly on Lotus' vast experience of single-seater and sports-car racing worldwide. Vacuum servo-assisted disc brakes appear all round, with fat tyres on neat, lightweight, cast-alloy wheels and very precise rack-and-pinion steering.

Unfortunately, in the Series 1 cars at least, the gearchange was not very good owing to the problems, common in mid-engined cars, of mating up a cockpit change with rear-mounted transmission while at the same time insulating the cockpit area from noise and vibration. There was body boom generated in the engine bay, and it took quite a while to sort these difficulties out to the customers' satisfaction. Finally it was achieved, with the Esprit Series 2.

In 1978 a turbocharged version of the pretty Esprit was developed by one of Lotus's major distributors, and so brought real power to a sports car worthy of the eighties.

Panther Six
1979, Great Britain

Bob Jankel established his Panther Westwinds company essentially to build what were virtual modern-day replicas of the SS100 pre-war sports car. They proved very successful, they were very well made and beautifully finished, and Jankel's company progressed to make all manner of replica-type sporting vehicles plus some high-quality special coachwork projects. This programme culminated in the series production of the Panther Lima GM-Detroit and Vauxhall-engined two-seat sports car. This was very much an evocation of the MG TC era, expressed in modern high-quality glass-fibre and based on a production-car chassis pan, engine, gearbox and running gear offering no spares and servicing problems.

Panther now wanted a flagship model for their newly broad range, and during 1976–77 Jankel was impressed by the performance on circuit of the six-wheeled Tyrrell Project 34 Grand Prix cars. He determined to make a sporting car to excel all others.

Panther installed side-by-side bench seating for three at most in the open cockpit of a mid-engined six-wheeled car of outstanding comfort and opulence. To achieve the stunning performance required Jankel chose a seven- or eight-litre American Cadillac V8 engine mated to a General Motors automatic transmission. What was more, he contracted Ak Miller–a prince of the Californian hot-rod movement–to fit twin Garrett AiResearch turbochargers to the V8 engine to boost it to 600 bhp.

The result could have been either stunning or frightening. In fact Panther adopted what they called 'softly-softly' ride control from Jaguar saloon suspension units and the Panther Six, as the car was christened, emerged as an incredibly comfortable device with tremendous power and performance potential both in a straight line and through corners. The author was the first journalist to drive it, and although underdeveloped it impressed him deeply with its bite under brakes and turning into corners. Unfortunately Panther found themselves crippled over supply of the special front tyres required, and production of the six-wheeler hung fire.

Porsche Turbo
1979, Germany

As the seventies reached their close undoubtedly the most potent sporting car generally available in the sports-car market was Porsche's Type 930 Turbo. This had evolved from the long-serving Porsche 911 family whose world-wide success in production trim was based on one of the most comprehensive and expensive competition programmes any major motor manufacturer has ever been involved in.

The turbocharged model was introduced at the Paris Salon of 1974, stunning all observers with its enormously wide tyres enclosed in massive fender cowls, its front air dam and prominent tail spoiler.

The flat-six-cylinder engine of the 911 family, as used in the Porsche Carrera model in three-litre unsupercharged form, had reached the end of its development and only supercharging promised a future for it. Porsche

Ultimate development of the 911 family: the Porsche Turbo, combining familiar looks with stunning performance.

chose to adopt exhaust-driven turbo-super-charging in which an impeller vane introduced into the exhaust stream is forced to revolve. Its spindle then drives a similar impeller in the induction side of a super-charger unit which then feeds the engine with mixture under pressure. This system had been developed by Porsche in competition from 1972; in the road-going Porsche Turbo 2 + 2 coupé the three-litre engine was boosted at a maximum of 121 lb per square inch pressure, and responded by producing an enormously reliable – and not uneconomical – 260 bhp at 5500 rpm. What was more important, the turbocharged engine gave an

incredibly wide power band which allowed the Porsche Turbo driver to outperform almost anything on the public road without wearing himself out by continual resort to the gear lever. The Turbo would potter happily about at 2000 rpm in top gear, but with the driver's foot hard down it would reach 50 mph from rest in a mere 3.6 seconds, 100 mph in 11.8 seconds and 125 mph in less than 20 seconds. Top speed was around 155 mph at 6000 rpm – but the brakes in these early cars had a hard time and it was not until the advent of the 3.3-litre Turbo version in September 1977 that the model finally received the brakes which its enormous performance really demanded.

De Lorean
1980, Great Britain

John Zachary De Lorean was a chief executive of the mighty General Motors Corporation – the world's largest private enterprise – until he suddenly decided to go his own way and build his own high-performance cars. Many others had done this before, but very few had ever succeeded. De Lorean was ambitious in an unusual way and set out to build a sporting car primarily for the American market which would break new ground in automotive technology.

He wanted a mid-engined two-seater car with outstanding styling, including gull-wing doors à la Mercedes 300SL; it would combine advanced safety features with good performance and fuel economy. Structurally the car was to employ a number of plastic processes for which De Lorean held US licences.

In December 1974 De Lorean and his chief engineer, Bill Collins, another ex-GM man, went to the Turin Motor Show in Italy to talk with the world's top stylists and Giorgetto Giugiaro was their choice as the man with the most attractive ideas.

Giugiaro consequently styled the De Lorean prototype which was built up to completion in

October 1976. A Ford V6 was contemplated initially as the power unit for this car but the first prototype was fitted with a 2.2-litre Citroen CX four-cylinder engine and trans-axle, while later cars were to use the Renault 30 power-train. This featured the alloy Peugeot/Renault/Volvo V6 engine which delivers about 120 bhp at 5500 rpm. This was good enough for a 0–60 mph acceleration time of about eight seconds and fuel economy of the order of 22 mpg in city driving and 29 mpg on longer runs. With all-independent suspension and four-wheel disc brakes the De Lorean was remarkable for its stainless-steel external panels, and the company initially planned to open a factory on a disused US military base in Puerto Rico once its plans had received sufficient financial backing from American institutions and private investors.

Subsequently, however, De Lorean was attracted to Ulster by British Government subsidies, and the development of his dream car was undertaken in collaboration with one of his major potential rivals, the Lotus Group.

The Sports Car Constructors

Many manufacturers in motoring history have built what might be described as 'sporting' cars. The list which follows tells who, what and when . . .

Nationalities are given according to convention as follows: A = Austria, AUS = Australia, CH = Switzerland, CZ = Czechoslovakia, D = Germany, E = Spain, F = France, GB = Great Britain, I = Italy, J = Japan, USA = United States, ZA = South Africa.

Abadal (E) 1912–14 *Some performance models*
Abarth (I) 1950–71 *All sporting cars, tuned saloons*
ABC (GB) 1920–29 *About 1500 made*
AC (GB) 1908 to date *See text*
Ader (F) 1900–07 *Clement Ader, pioneer aviator*
Adler (D) 1900–39 *Today's typewriter company*
Aero (CZ) 1929–47 *Czechoslovakian sports cars*
Aero Minor (CZ) 1946–52 *Ran a car at Le Mans 1949*
AF (GB) 1971–72 *Morgan 3-wheeler 'replica'*
Aga (D) 1919–28 *Ran in Targa Florio 1924*
Airphibian (USA) 1950–56 *Ultimate sports car, it could fly!*
Alco (USA) 1905–13 *Locomotive company, 1909–10 cars won Vanderbilt Cup race*
Alcyon (F) 1906–28 *Well-known in Voiturette racing*
Alda (F) 1912–22 *'Ah, la Délicieuse Automobile' . . .*
Alexis (GB) 1961– *Trials specials, then single-seaters*
Alfa Romeo (I) 1910 to date *See text*
Allard (GB) 1937–60 *See text*
Alphi (F) 1929–31 *Only four built, Le Mans car 1929*
Alpine (F) 1955 to date *See text*
Alta (GB) 1931–54 *Geoffrey Taylor's 'hobby'*
Alvis (GB) 1920–67 *Fine motor cars*
Amédée Bollée (F) 1885–1922 *Pioneer sporting cars*
American Austin (USA) 1930–31 *Bantam Austin 7 derivative*
Amilcar (F) 1921–39 *See text*
Anagasti (ARG) 1911–15 *Argentinian enthusiast's cars*
Anzani (I) 1923–24 *Fast light cars*
Apollo (D) 1910–26 *German sports cars*
Aquila-Italiana (I) 1906–17 *Up-market Italian*
Arab (GB) 1926–28 *Reid Railton designed*
Aries (F) 1903–38 *Up-market Frenchman*
ASA (I) 1962–67 *Built baby Ferrari*
Aston Martin (GB) 1922 to date *See text*
Atalanta (GB) 1937–39 *Advanced technology didn't sell*
ATS (I) 1962–64 *Poor attempt to out-Ferrari Ferrari*
Auburn (USA) 1900–37 *See text*
Audi (D) 1910–35 *Successful early trial cars, current marque re-formed in 1965*
Austin-Healey (GB) 1953–71 *See text*
Austro-Daimler (A) 1899–36 *Austria's most famous*
Ballot (F) 1919–32 *See Racing Cars, companion vol.*
Bandini (I) 1947–56 *Small Italian sports-racer*
Batten (GB) 1935–38 *Stark Ford V8-based sports cars*
Béchereau (F) 1924–25 *Light car by originator of 'monocoque' aircraft fuselage construction*
Bédélia (F) 1910–25 *See text*
Bentley (GB) 1920–30 *See text*
Benz (D) 1885–1926 *Pioneer merged with Daimler 1926*
Berkeley (GB) 1956–61 *See text*
Berliet (F) 1895–1939 *Models included fast roadsters*
Beverley-Barnes (GB) 1924–31 *High-quality individual 'specials'*
Bignan (F) 1918–30 *Genuinely sporting cars*
Biota (GB) 1968–BMC *Mini-based sports special*
Bizzarini (I) 1965–69 *By ex-Ferrari GTO engineer*
BMW (D) 1928 to date *See text*

BNC (F) 1923–31 *French sporting voiturettes*
Bobsy (USA) 1962– *American sports-racing cars*
Bocar (USA) 1958–61 *Sports cars using US engines*
Borgward (D) 1939–61 *Distinctly sporting German*
Brabham (GB) 1962–71 *True racers, some two-seaters*
Brasier (F) 1897–1930 *See Racing Cars, companion vol.*
Bristol (GB) 1947 to date *Up-market advanced sporting cars*
British Salmson (GB) 1934–39 *French-licensed*
Bucciali (F) 1923–33 *Unconventional and expensive*
Buckler (GB) 1947–62 *Built-it-yourself specials*
Bugatti (F) *See text*
Caban (F) 1926–32 *Built by Yves Giraud-Cabantous, racing driver*
Calthorpe (GB) 1904–32 *Some sporting models*
Cannon (GB) 1953 *One-man-built trials specials*
Case (USA) 1910–27 *From agricultural machinery works*
Cegga (CH) 1960–67 *Swiss specialists*
Ceirano (I) 1919–31 *Range included sporting cars*
CGV-Charron (F) 1901–30 *Racing drivers' partnership*
Chadwick (USA) 1904–16 *Lee Chadwick's enthusiast concern achieved high production*
Chenard-Walcker (F) 1901–46 *Won first Le Mans, 1923*
Chevrolet (USA) 1911 to date *See text*
Chevron (GB) 1961 to date *Sports-racing cars*
Chiribiri (I) 1913–27 *Small sports cars renowned in Italy*
Cisitalia (I) 1946–65 *See text*
Clément-Bayard (F) 1899–1922 *French tourers*
CMN (I) 1919–23 *Enzo Ferrari was a works tester!*
Coldwell (GB) 1967– *Mini-based grand touring cars*
Connaught (GB) 1949–57 *Sports cars led to Grands Prix*
Cooper (GB) 1948–69 *Some sports cars amongst the racers*
Cord (USA) 1929–37 *Strikingly modern performance cars*
Cottin-Desgouttes (F) 1905–33 *French 'cad's car'*
Crespelle (F) 1906–23 *French sporting cars*
Crosley (USA) 1939–52 *Crosley Hot-Shot good two-seater*
Crossle (GB) 1959– *Ulster sports-racing cars*
Cunningham (USA) 1951–55 *Le Mans project begat roadsters*
Darracq (F) 1896–1920 *Early French sports-racing marque*
DB (F) 1938–61 *French high-performance 'specials'*
De Bruyne (GB) 1968 *Took over Gordon-Keeble GT*
De Dietrich (F) 1897–1905 *Early French sporting marque*
De Dion-Bouton (F) 1883–1932 *Included racing success amid conservatism*
Delage (F) 1905–54 *An honoured marque*
Delahaye (F) 1894–54 *See text*
Dellow (GB) 1949–59 *Sporting trial specials*
Derby (F) 1921–36 *French, notably front-drives*
De Tomaso (I) 1959 to date *Argentinian-founded*
Diatto (I) 1905–27 *Set Maserati brothers on their way*
Disbrow (USA) 1917–18 *Racing driver's two-seaters*
DKW (D) 1928–66 *Included sporting models*
Duesenberg (USA) 1920–37 *Up-market performance marque*
Elva (GB) 1955–68 *Sports-racing cars, one roadster*
EMW (EDR) 1945–55 *East German BMW works*
Eric-Campbell (GB) 1919–26 *British sporting car*
Excelsior (B) 1903–32 *Built GP cars amongst range*
Facel Vega (F) 1954–64 *Costly Franco-American*

Fairthorpe (GB) 1954– *Small-series sports range*
Ferrari (I) 1940 to date *See text*
Fiat (I) 1899 to date *See text*
Fitch (USA) 1949–51 *Racing driver's marque*
Ford (USA) 1903 to date *See text*
Frazer Nash (GB) 1924–60 *British and race-bred*
Georges Irat (F) 1921–46 *Small French sports cars*
Giannini (I) 1920– *Tuned Fiats, own sports-racers*
Gilbern (GB) 1959– *Wales's sporting marque*
Ginetta (GB) 1957– *Suffolk's sporting marque*
GN (GB) 1910–25 *See text*
Gobron-Brillie (F) 1898–1930 *Fine French performance and racing cars*
Gordano (GB) 1946–50 *Bristolian project for enthusiasts*
Gordini (F) 1951–57 *Noble but under-financed Frenchman*
Gordon-Keeble (GB) 1960–67 *Fine but under-financed Briton*
Grégoire (F) 1903–24 *Numerous sporting models*
GSM (ZA/GB) 1958–66 *Anglo-South African GTs*
Healey (GB) 1946–54 *See text*
Hermes (B) 1909 *Racing driver's sporting car*
Hispano-Suiza (E/F) 1904–44 *See text*
Horch (D) 1900–39 *See text*
Hotchkiss (F) 1903–55 *American's French ordnance works-cum-motor company*
HRG (GB) 1936–56 *See text*
HWM (GB) 1950–56 *Some Jaguar sports-racers*
Imperia (B) 1906–49 *Products included a race winner*
Invicta (GB) 1925–38 *Fine British sporting car*
Iso (I) 1962– *Italian up-market exoticar*
Isotta-Fraschini (I) 1900–49 *See text*
Itala (I) 1904–34 *Fabled Italian marque*
Jaguar (GB) 1945 to date *See text*
Jensen (GB) 1936–75 *Fine British marque*
Jowett (GB) 1906–54 *Built advanced sporting cars*
Kieft (GB) 1950–61 *Specialized sports-racing cars*
Kurtis (USA) 1948–55 *Indy specialist-built roadsters*
La Buire (F) 1904–30 *Dignified French marque*
Lagonda (GB) 1906–63 *Fine British cars from American*
Lambert (F) 1926–53 *Included sporting models*
Lamborghini (I) 1963– *Up-market tractor manufacturer*
Lanchester (GB) 1895–56 *See text*
Lancia (I) 1906 to date *See text*
La Perle (F) 1913–27 *French small sporting cars*
Lea-Francis (GB) 1904–60 *Stop-go production*
Lenham (GB) 1968 to date *Sports-racing specialists*
Lester (GB) 1949–55 *Sports-racing specialist*
Ligier (F) 1969 to date *French GT and Formula 1 specialists*
Lion-Peugeot (F) 1906–13 *French voiturette kings*
Lister (GB) 1954–59 *Bristol and Jaguar-engined racers*
Lola (GB) 1958 to date *See text*
Lombard (F) 1927–29 *Sporting voiturettes*
Lotus (GB) 1952 to date *See text*
Lozier (USA) 1905–17 *Great American sportsman*
Marendaz (GB) 1926–36 *Successful sportsman*
Marmon (USA) 1902–33 *Excellent American marque*
Maserati (I) 1926 to date *See text*
Mathid (D) 1898–50 *Alsatian enthusiasm*
Matich (AUS) 1965– *Australian enthusiasm*
Matra (F) 1965 to date *See text*
Mazda (J) 1960 to date *Japanese rotary-engined*
McLaren (GB) 1964 to date *New Zealander's racing team*
Mercedes-Benz (D) 1926 to date *See text*
Metallurgique (B) 1898–1928 *Fine Belgian sporting marque*
MG (GB) 1924 to date *See text*

Miller (USA) 1915–32 *American genius in a golden age*
Moretti (I) 1945 to date *Italian small cars*
Morgan (GB) 1910 to date *See text*
Mors (F) 1895–1943 *Legendary French marque*
Nacional Pescara (E) 1929–32 *Aristocratic Spaniard*
Napier (GB) 1900–24 *Quality Briton*
Nardi (I) 1947–56 *Enthusiastic Italian*
Nash (USA) 1917–57 *Multi-national enthusiasm*
Nazzaro (I) 1911–23 *Racing driver's dream*
OM (I) 1918–34 *See text*
OSCA (I) 1947–67 *Maserati brothers' last resting place*
Panther (GB) 1972–80 *Classic-styled replicars*
Peerless (GB) 1957–60 *Triumph TR3-based GT*
Pegaso (E) 1951–58 *See text*
Piper (GB) 1966– *Striking super-low GTs*
Porsche (D) 1948 to date *See text*
Probe (GB) 1969–71 *Another super-low GT*
Railton (GB) 1933–49 *Reid Railton's own marque*
Reliant (GB) 1952 to date *Four-wheeled GTs out of three-wheeler predecessors*
René Bonnet (F) 1962–64 *French specialist sold to Matra*
RGS-Atalanta (GB) 1947–58 *Specialist built on Atalanta base*
Riley (GB) 1898–1969 *See text*
Rohr (D) 1928–35 *Sensationally advanced sporting cars*
Rolland-Pilain (F) 1906–31 *French high technology*
Salmson (F) 1921–57 *See text*
SARA (F) 1923–30 *Air-cooled performance car*
Sbarro (CH) 1971 to date *Swiss build anything up-market*
Serenissima (I) 1965–70 *Short-lived successor to ATS*
Shelby-American (USA) 1962–70 *See text (AC Cobra)*
Siata (I) 1949–70 *Multinational GTs*
Simca (F) 1935 to date *With Gordini's help made racers*
Simplex (USA) 1907–17 *Big American took sporting honours*
Singer (GB) 1905–70 *Small Briton took sporting honours*
Sizaire-Naudin (F) 1905–21 *See text*
Squire (GB) 1934–36 *See text*
SS (GB) 1931–45 *See text*
Stanguellini (I) 1946–66 *Small Italian sporting and racing cars*
Steyr (A) 1920–40 *Fine Austrian marque*
Straker-Squire (GB) 1906–26 *Advanced sporting vintagent*
Stutz (USA) 1911–35 *Legendary American sports and racing cars*
Sunbeam (GB) 1953 to date *See text*
Talbot (GB) 1903–38 *See text*
Tatra (CZ) 1923 to date *High-speed Czech*
Terrier (GB) 1959–61 *British club racing specialist*
Thornycroft (GB) 1903–13 *Serious concern dabbled in racing*
Th. Schneider (F) 1910–31 *Energetic race promotion for road designs*
Tojeiro (GB) 1952–62 *Sports-racing car specialist*
Tornado (GB) 1958–64 *Another British special*
Tracta (F) 1926–34 *Fine French front-drive*
Trident (GB) 1965– *British GT specials*
Triumph (GB) 1923 to date *See text*
Turner (GB) 1951–66 *British sporting specialist*
TVR (GB) 1954 to date *Apparently immortal specialist*
U2 (GB) 1959 to date *The ultimate club-racing cars*
Vale (GB) 1932–36 *British sports cars*
Vauxhall (GB) 1903 to date *See text*
Veritas (D) 1948–53 *See text*
Voisin (F) 1919–39 *Aviation-minded innovation*
Wanderer (D) 1911–39 *High-minded German*
Warwick (GB) 1960–62 *Peerless transmogrified*
Winton (USA) 1897–24 *American pioneer marque*
Wolseley (GB) 1899–75 *Included sporting models*

Index

ACKNOWLEDGEMENTS

Picture Research: Tim Auger and Elizabeth Rudoff

Photographs: AC Cars 57; British Leyland 48, 49 *(bottom);* Neil Bruce 78; Classic Car 54, 55; Datsun 82; General Motors 22, 23 *(top)*, 62 *(both)*, 63; Geoff Goddard 58; London Art Technical 12, 23 *(bottom)*, 56 *(both)*, 66, 69 *(both)*, 71, 73, 84; Matra 13; MG Car Club 61; National Motor Museum 10, 11 *(both)*, 24, 25, 26, 27, 28, 29 *(all)*, 32, 36, 37, 38, 40, 42, 43, 44, 45, 49 *(top)*, 52, 53, 59, 63 *(centre)*, 71 *(centre)*, 77; Renault 8; Philip Young 72; Neil Bruce cover